OUT of the BOX

JEMMA WESTING

OUT of the BOX

DK

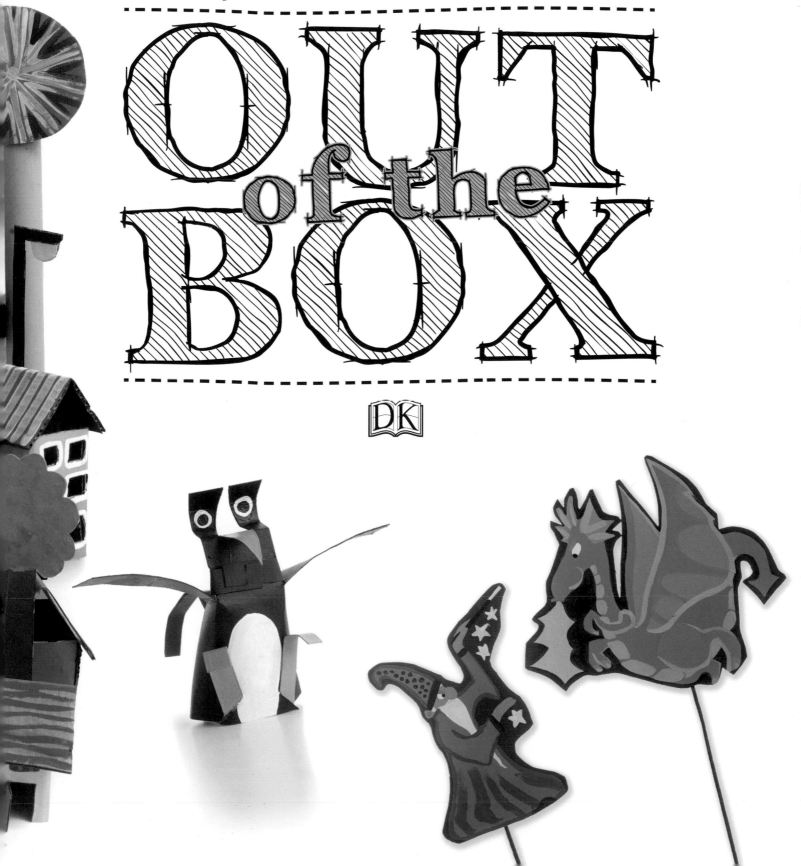

Senior art editor Amy Child
Project editors Suhel Ahmed, Lili Bryant
Designers Laura Gardner, Mik Gates, Alex Lloyd, Sean Ross
Editors Sarah Edwards, Laura Sandford
Design assistant Edward Byrne

Managing editor Daniel Mills
Managing art editor Anna Hall
Producer, pre-production David Almond
Producer Anna Vallarino
Jacket design development manager Sophia MTT
Jacket editor Claire Gell
Senior jacket designer Mark Cavanagh
Jacket designer Jemma Westing

Publisher Andrew Macintyre
Associate publishing director Liz Wheeler
Art director Karen Self
Publishing director Jonathan Metcalf

Author and model creator Jemma Westing
Photographer Dave King
Photography art direction Jane Ewart
Illustrator Edward Byrne

First published in Great Britain in 2017
by Dorling Kindersley Limited
80 Strand, London, WC2R 0RL

Copyright © 2017 Dorling Kindersley Limited
A Penguin Random House Company
2 4 6 8 10 9 7 5 3 1
001-299504-Mar/2017

Printed and bound in China

A WORLD OF IDEAS:
SEE ALL THERE IS TO KNOW

www.dk.com

 IMPORTANT NOTE TO PARENTS

The activities in this book may require adult help and supervision, depending
on your child's age and ability. Always ensure that your child uses tools that
are appropriate to their age, and offer help and supervision as necessary
to keep them safe. The publisher cannot accept any liability for injury, loss,
or damage to any property or user following suggestions in this book.

CONTENTS

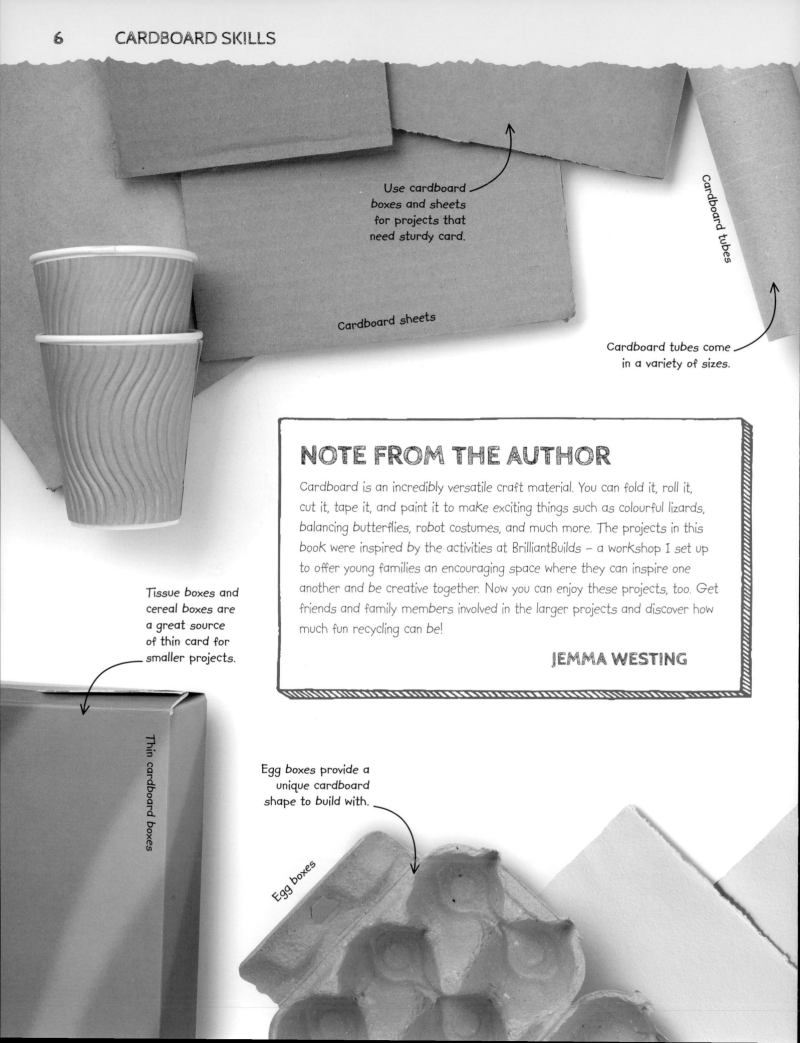

Use cardboard boxes and sheets for projects that need sturdy card.

Cardboard sheets

Cardboard tubes

Cardboard tubes come in a variety of sizes.

NOTE FROM THE AUTHOR

Cardboard is an incredibly versatile craft material. You can fold it, roll it, cut it, tape it, and paint it to make exciting things such as colourful lizards, balancing butterflies, robot costumes, and much more. The projects in this book were inspired by the activities at BrilliantBuilds – a workshop I set up to offer young families an encouraging space where they can inspire one another and be creative together. Now you can enjoy these projects, too. Get friends and family members involved in the larger projects and discover how much fun recycling can be!

JEMMA WESTING

Tissue boxes and cereal boxes are a great source of thin card for smaller projects.

Thin cardboard boxes

Egg boxes provide a unique cardboard shape to build with.

Egg boxes

Coloured envelopes are a good source of coloured paper.

GETTING STARTED

The projects in this book use cardboard packaging that you can find lying around the house. The book will show you how to make recycling fun by building exciting, interactive models that you can play with afterwards. You'll find a list of the materials and tools required at the start of each project. Once you have everything you need, simply follow the instructions and see your wonderful creations come together!

Tracing paper

White paper

TYPES OF CARDBOARD

Cardboard comes in many different forms, shapes, and sizes. A box provides a great structure for making many of the models, and cardboard tubes (taken from rolls of wrapping paper and paper towels) provide ready-made cylindrical shapes. Moulded cardboard, such as egg boxes, shoe formers, and furniture corner caps offer more interesting shapes, and cereal boxes are an ideal source of thin card. Try not to throw away any scraps, but store them in a special "off-cuts" box, as they might come in handy for another project.

IGNORE THE PRINT

Cereal and tissue boxes will have designs and logos on them. Don't worry. You can paint over these when you decorate your model, or you might decide to keep them because they give your build a unique appeal.

OTHER BITS AND PIECES

Some projects require additional material besides cardboard, usually for adding the final touches. Once again, these should be easy to find, but make your own alternatives if you are struggling to find them.

Use tracing paper or thin white paper to copy templates for making more complex shapes.

INSIDE YOUR
TOOLBOX

The great thing about building out of cardboard is that you don't need to invest in specialized tools and equipment. Everything you need is probably in your stationery drawer already, so you should be ready to start right away. It is important that you use the right kind of tape in each project, and have scissors, rulers, and paintbrushes of varying sizes so you can make the smaller decorative builds as well as the large-scale models.

Decorate your models with glitter to add sparkle to them.

Check which type of tape you need before starting a project.

Double-sided tape

Sticky tape

Scissors

Thread

Pencil

Strong tape

Glue

String

Rulers

Coloured pencils

Paints

Paintbrushes

Use a broad paintbrush to decorate your larger models.

Felt pens offer an easier option for colouring in intricate patterns.

Felt pens

Use acrylic paints to decorate your models.

Sticky tack

Paints

CARDBOARD SKILLS

The different ways of cutting, shaping, and connecting cardboard are all very similar to each other, so once you have learned the basic principles, you can apply them to all the projects. The projects get more challenging as the book goes on, so if you're a beginner, start with the first project and see your skills grow as you work your way through.

Each project *begins* with a panel that includes a *useful* tip and a dial that tells you how challenging the project is.

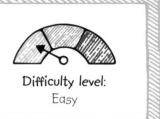

Nice and quick!
Make several for an eye-catching display.

Difficulty level:
Easy

DRAWING
You'll mostly be drawing straight lines and basic shapes. For circles you can draw around a cup, plate, or any other circular object.

CUTTING
Use a small pair of scissors to cut thin card and more intricate shapes, and larger scissors to cut thick pieces of cardboard.

A sharp pencil is a great tool for piercing holes.

Sticky tack

MAKING HOLES
For neat, round holes, pierce cardboard with the tip of a pencil with a rubber or sticky tack on the other side so you don't poke the surface below.

CUTTING OUT SHAPES
To cut out a shape, use a sharp pencil to pierce the cardboard, while holding sticky tack on the other side to protect your fingers. Then cut the shape out.

ROLLING

To make a tube, lay your cardboard piece on a flat surface and roll it into the size you want. Then trim off any excess card and tape the edge to secure the shape.

BENDING

You can use your hands to bend cardboard into all kinds of curved shapes and then secure it with tape. Take your time when you bend thick cardboard.

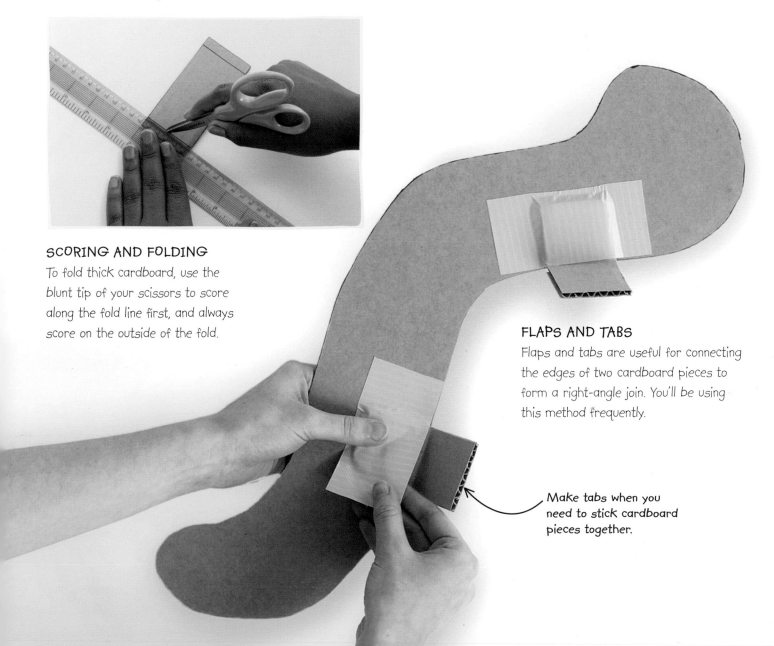

SCORING AND FOLDING

To fold thick cardboard, use the blunt tip of your scissors to score along the fold line first, and always score on the outside of the fold.

FLAPS AND TABS

Flaps and tabs are useful for connecting the edges of two cardboard pieces to form a right-angle join. You'll be using this method frequently.

Make tabs when you need to stick cardboard pieces together.

TAPING

Sticky tape is fine for the small projects, but strong tape is more suitable for making the larger builds because the joins need to be stronger.

GLUING

For creating neat, invisible joins in the smaller decorative builds, use glue instead of tape, especially to stick card onto card.

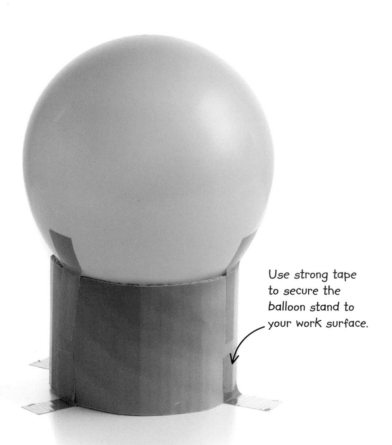

Use strong tape to secure the balloon stand to your work surface.

BALLOON HEAD STAND

For the projects that involve making hats, masks, and headdresses, you can either build directly around your head, which might be tricky without help, or create a head shape to build on. If you decide to use the balloon stand featured throughout the book, blow up a balloon to roughly the size of your head and place it on a cardboard base that is about as wide as your neck.

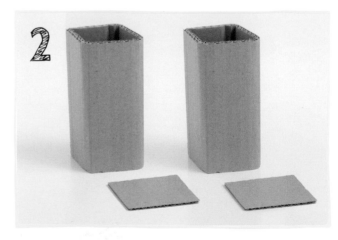

MAKE YOUR OWN BOX

If you can't find the right size box for any of the projects, you can always make your own box. First, cut out a cardboard rectangle, fold it to make a rectangular tube, and secure it with tape. Then cut out two cardboard squares and tape them over the ends of the tube.

TEMPLATES FOR TRACING

The templates at the back of the book are there to help you draw more complex shapes. If you need to use a template for a project, the instructions will tell you which page to find it on. Turn to the relevant page, trace the template onto plain paper or tracing paper, and cut it out. Then, lay the paper cut-out on cardboard and draw around it for the exact shape you need. Occasionally, you'll be instructed to flip the template over to make a symmetrical shape.

DEALING WITH MISHAPS!

If you accidentally tear a bit of cardboard or cut it too short, you could tape it together, glue it back on, or just remake the piece. Similarly, if you don't like the colour you've used for decorating, wait until it's dry and then paint over it. Mistakes will happen, but don't let that put you off – work through them!

NOW TRY THIS

Most projects in this book have a section at the end called "Now Try This", which will show you alternative ways to decorate your models, or things you can add to them to make them extra special. You can even combine parts of two or more different projects! For example, this book will show you how to turn your penguins from the Penguin Family (page 88) into competitors in the game Racing Rabbits (page 44).

Paint the racetrack in icy colours.

Add a paper tube to your penguins so they can join in the racing game.

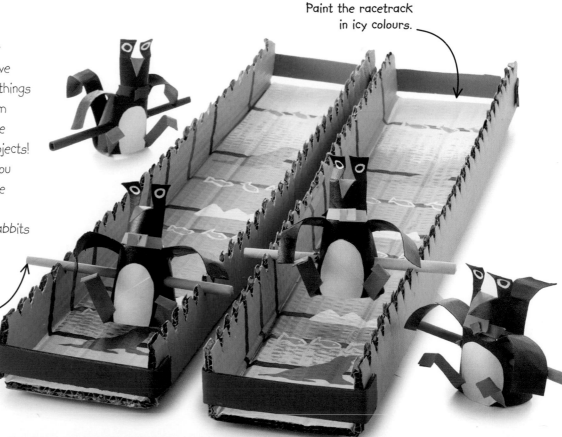

TUBE OWLS

Did you know that there are around 200 species of owl? Now you can make your very own collection of cute, colourful owls. Give them huge eyes to help them spot their prey, and pointy claws so they can perch in the trees!

Press the top of the tube down to give your owl pointy ears.

HOW TO MAKE
TUBE OWLS

It's really quick and easy to transform a cardboard tube into one of these lovable owls. Making a few simple cuts into the tube will give your owl feet, a beak, and wings!

All you need to do is **cut, fold, and paint** a cardboard tube.

Difficulty level:
Easy

YOU WILL NEED

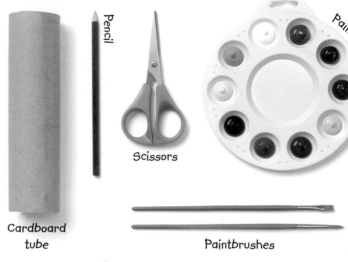

Pencil

Paints

Scissors

Cardboard tube

Paintbrushes

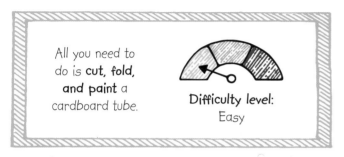
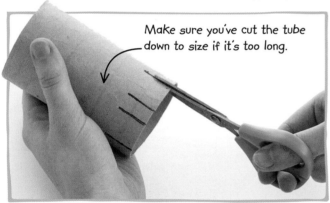

Make sure you've cut the tube down to size if it's too long.

1 First, make the owl's **feet**. Gently flatten your tube and draw four short lines, spaced apart as shown. Make cuts along all four lines.

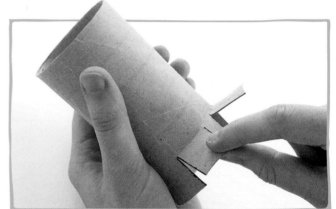

2 The cuts that you have made will create two flaps. Fold these flaps outwards and away from the tube to make the owl's feet.

3 Now that you have folded the feet over, trim around the base of the tube. Cut away any card that is below the level of the feet.

Draw zig-zags for claws.

4 To finish making the feet, draw zig-zag lines on the end of each foot. Carefully cut along the lines to give your owl nice pointy **claws**.

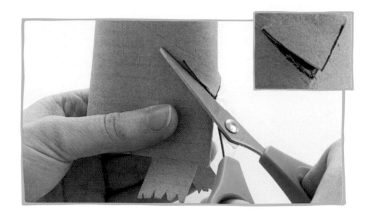

5 Next, make the owl's **beak**. Using a pencil, carefully draw a V shape in the centre of the tube.

6 Squeeze the tube a little to help you cut along the two lines. Then prise out the beak and gently fold it up away from the tube, making sure it doesn't tear.

The pressed-down ends of the tube give your owl its ears.

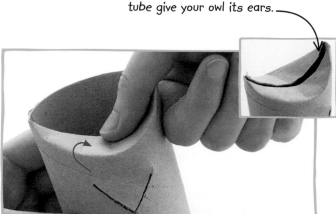

7 To make the owl's **head**, press down the front and back edges of the top of the tube. Then fold them inwards to form a curved head shape.

NOW TRY THIS
Add **wings** to your owls. To do this, cut V shapes on either side of the tube, following the instructions in **step 6**.

Add feather details.

Gently curve the wings away from the body.

8 Finally, draw the **features** of your owl with a pencil. Then paint them on in bright colours, using a fine paintbrush for any detailed decoration.

RING TOSS CHALLENGE

Do you love fairground games, but hardly ever get to play them? Why not create your own ring toss game at home? Invite your friends to play, then work on perfecting your aim.

Try to throw all the rings over the pins.

Make the pins different shapes and sizes.

You can make the target board as big and complex as you want to.

HOW TO MAKE
RING TOSS CHALLENGE

The game is very easy to make and will provide hours of fun for you and your friends. Make sure you store the board inside so you can use it again and again!

Sticky tack

Large cardboard sheet

Ruler

Scissors

Pencil

Paints

Paintbrushes

1 To make your **target board**, draw the outline of the board on a sheet of cardboard and add sloping flaps on either side. These will make the board stand up.

Make sure the pins are far enough apart and small enough for the rings to fit over them.

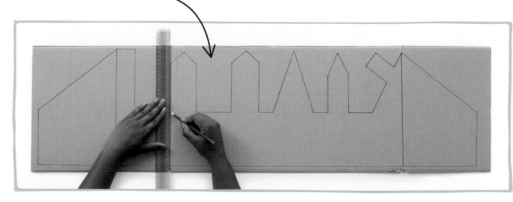

2 Carefully cut out your target board with scissors. Make sure you don't cut off the sloping flaps!

Don't cut here.

Don't cut here.

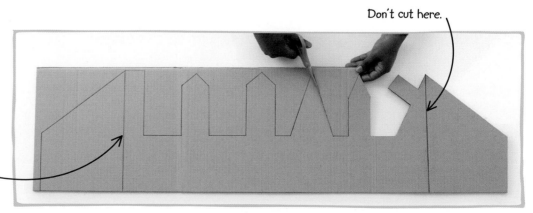

3 Use a ruler and the tips of your scissors to score both sloping ends of the target board. Fold them back to create flaps to stand your board up.

Score here, too.

4 It's time to decorate the board. Paint the stand one colour and each pin a different colour, so they stand out.

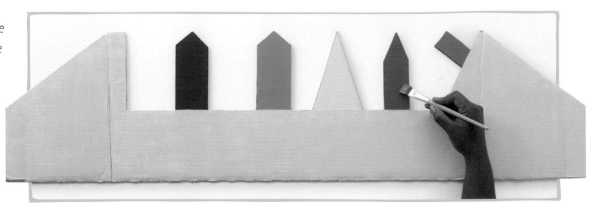

Make sure the flaps are stable and the stand is not near anything fragile.

5 Place your ring template from page 134 on a piece of cardboard and draw around it. Repeat the process to draw as many rings as you want.

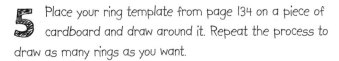

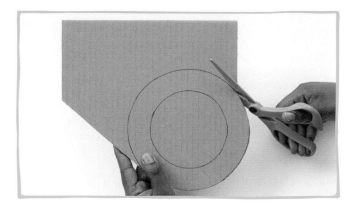

6 Cut the rings out. Cut around the outside first, then place the sticky tack underneath, pierce the centre of the ring with a sharp pencil, and cut it out.

7 Paint the rings and leave them to dry. You can make them any colour you like. You could even add patterns like stripes or dots to your set.

8 The ring toss board is ready. Find some friends and try it out. If you want to make things competitive, paint different point values on the pins and see who can reach 100 points first.

Be careful not to bend the pins over when you set the stand up.

Stand about five paces away and try to throw the rings over the pins.

BALANCING BUTTERFLIES

These butterflies are not only beautiful but they can also balance on a stick or on the tip of your finger! Discover the secret behind their gravity-defying act and put them on display to impress your friends.

HOW TO MAKE
BALANCING BUTTERFLIES

Use the template on page 135 to draw the butterfly and decorate it with bright colours and pretty patterns. Once finished, add sticky tack to each wing, then pick up the butterfly and watch it balance on the tip of your finger!

A **quick and easy** project. Make several butterflies for a stunning display!

Difficulty level: Easy

YOU WILL NEED

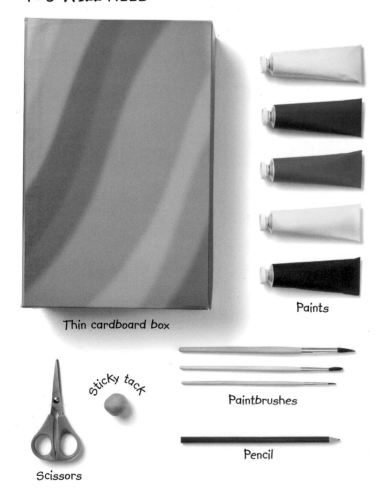

Thin cardboard box

Paints

Sticky tack

Paintbrushes

Pencil

Scissors

1 Using a pair of scissors, cut out a large rectangle of thin card. The front or back panel of a cereal box is the ideal size.

2 Lay your **butterfly wing** template from page 135 on the card and draw around it, leaving room to draw the other half of the butterfly.

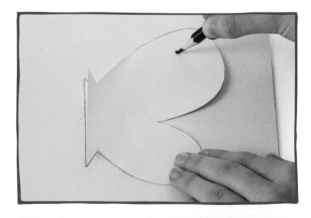

3 Put the tip of your pencil on the dot on the template, twist and push down hard to pierce the template and make a dot on the card below.

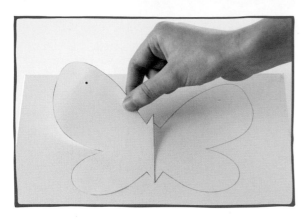

4 Flip the template over and draw around it to complete the butterfly shape. Then push your pencil tip into the hole and mark a dot on this wing too.

5 Carefully cut out your butterfly. The wings need to be symmetrical for your butterfly to balance, so cut as close to the lines as possible.

Carefully push a pencil through the middle of the sticky tack.

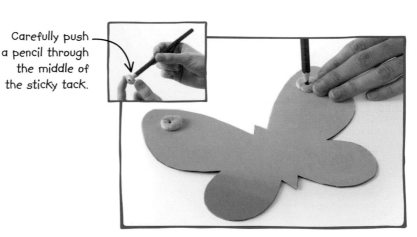

6 Now use brightly coloured paint to decorate the side of the butterfly without the two dots, adding beautiful patterns. Let the paint dry.

7 Roll two identical discs of sticky tack. Make a hole in the middle of each one with a pencil. Then use the pencil tip to line up the hole in each disc with the dot on the wing and fix it on.

8 Your butterfly is ready! Rest it on a point (like a stick, table corner, or the end of your finger) and watch it perform its awesome balancing act!

If your butterfly doesn't balance at first, make tiny adjustments to the positions of the sticky tack and try again.

Paint your board in a dark colour so your monsters stand out.

FEED THE MONSTERS

These monsters are ready for their dinner, and it's up to you to feed them! Create a huge board full of brightly coloured monsters with wide open mouths and sharp teeth. Then put your skills to the test and see how many monsters you can feed in a minute, or challenge a friend to see who can feed the most monsters.

FEED ME!

HOW TO MAKE
FEED THE MONSTERS

You'll need a huge sheet of cardboard for this project, so you can fill it with lots of hungry monsters. Make sure you also have enough cardboard to make two identical stand pieces, so that your board stays upright when you feed the monsters.

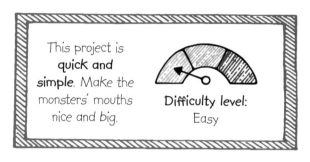

This project is **quick and simple**. Make the monsters' mouths nice and big.

Difficulty level: Easy

YOU WILL NEED

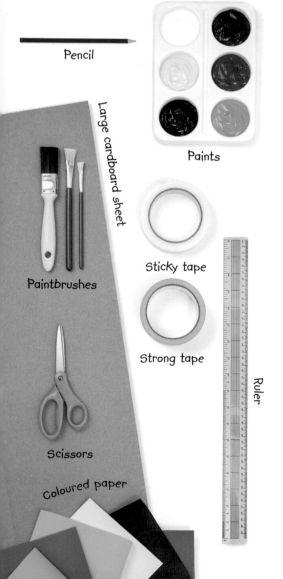

Pencil

Paints

Large cardboard sheet

Paintbrushes

Sticky tape

Strong tape

Scissors

Ruler

Coloured paper

1 On a large sheet of cardboard, draw lots of **monster faces** with wide open mouths and sharp teeth.

2 Carefully cut out holes where you have drawn the monsters' **mouths**. You might want to ask an adult to help.

Draw this horizontal line on both pieces for your stand.

3 Make the **stand** for your board. Take a square piece of cardboard and draw three lines on it as shown above.

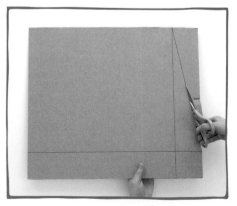

4 Cut along the diagonal line. Then, use your first stand piece as a template to create another.

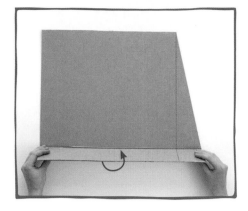

5 Score along the horizontal lines on both stand pieces to make tabs. Fold the tabs upwards.

6 Tape the tabs to each side of the board at the back. The diagonal edge of each stand piece should touch the floor.

7 To make your **paper balls**, scrunch up coloured paper into tight balls and wrap them in sticky tape.

8 Decorate your **board** and leave the paint to dry. Then stand it upright and you're ready to play!

Paint your monsters in *bold* colours.

NOW TRY THIS

Make one big monster by cutting a single monster mouth out of a cardboard box. Take the rings from the Ring Toss Challenge on page 21, and try to feed the monster yummy hoops. Use more card to add arms or hair if you like.

Paint the whole box.

Use more card to add details to your mega monster.

Cut out one big hole for the mouth.

FUNKY FLOWERS

This beautiful spray of bright, exotic flowers makes a fantastic decoration for your desk or windowsill. Or you can use them to make a hanging garland to bring colour to any room.

HOW TO MAKE
FUNKY FLOWERS

These flowers have three rings of petals: two made from a cardboard tube, and one cut from a template. The more evenly spaced the petals are, the neater your flowers will look, so measure and cut carefully.

A **quick project** that won't take up too much time or space!

Difficulty level: Easy

YOU WILL NEED

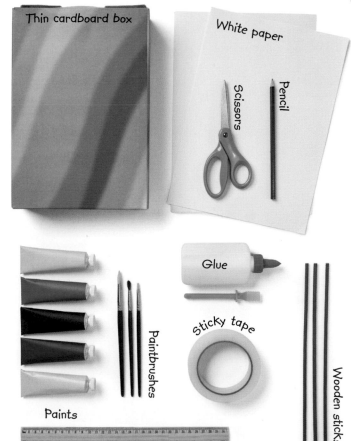

Thin cardboard box

White paper

Scissors

Pencil

Glue

Paintbrushes

Sticky tape

Wooden sticks

Paints

Ruler

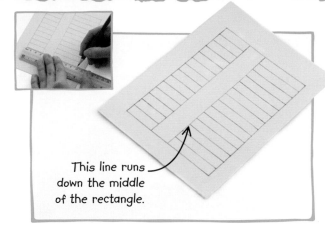

This line runs down the middle of the rectangle.

1 Use a pencil and ruler to draw the shape shown above on a piece of card. Make sure the rectangular strips are longer on one side of the piece than on the other side.

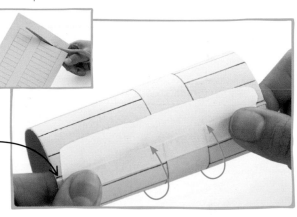

Line up the end with the nearest pencil line.

2 Cut out the rectangle, then roll it into a tube with the pencil lines facing out. Use sticky tape to hold the tube together.

Avoid cutting into the central gap.

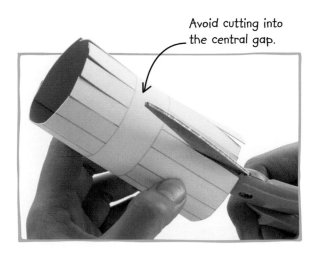

3 Use scissors to cut along the lines on each side of the tube. Be careful not to cut into the gap in the middle, or your flower will fall apart.

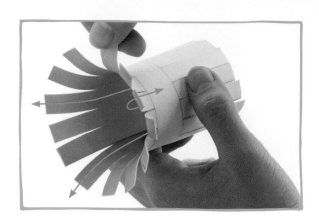

Fold here.

4 Gently bend the shorter set of strips outwards, so they form curves. These will become the **middle ring of petals** on your flower.

5 To create the **inner ring of petals**, push the longer strips through the tube so that they stick out at the other side. Fold the bases of the strips along the rim to keep them in place.

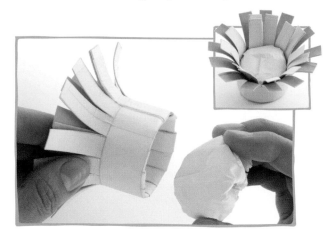

6 Screw a piece of paper up into a tight ball, then wedge it securely into the centre of the tube. You may need to add a little glue to the outside of the ball of paper to hold it in place.

7 To make the **outer ring of petals**, copy the petal template from page 135 onto a piece of thin card. Turn the template over, then draw around it again to make a complete ring of petals.

8 Use scissors to cut out the complete outer ring of petals. Don't cut down the middle!

9 To fix your flower together, put a dab of glue in the centre of your outer petal shape, then stick the rest of the flower securely on top.

10 Press down on the ball of paper in the centre of your flower to make sure all the pieces are securely stuck together.

11 Now it's time to paint your flower. Choose a main colour for each section, then add details and patterns on top.

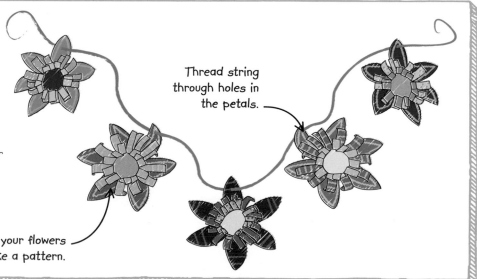

Look at pictures of real flowers for inspiration.

Try using a vibrant colour for the centre of the flower.

12 To make the **stalk**, use sticky tape to fix a stick or straw to the back of your flower. Your brilliant bloom is now ready to display in a vase or flowerbed.

NOW TRY THIS

Instead of putting your flowers on stalks, try creating a beautiful floral garland. Make five or six flowers and decorate them any way you like for an eye-catching garland! Then use a pencil to pierce a small hole in one of the outer petals on each flower. Thread a length of string through the holes and tie the ends together to complete your garland.

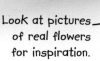

Thread string through holes in the petals.

Arrange your flowers to make a pattern.

CARDBOARD THEATRE

Put on an amazing show in your very own puppet theatre! Transform a cardboard sheet into a beautiful, old-fashioned theatre with a wooden floor and a colourful stage. Then, push your imagination to its limits and create an all-star cast of characters to bring your story to life.

Add trees from Cardville City (page 94) and towers from the Adventure Castle (page 80) to make a three-dimensional scene.

Make dragons, wizards, or any characters you like for your show!

CARDBOARD THEATRE

To make this traditional puppet theatre, you'll be turning a sheet of cardboard into a stage. Then, once you've painted your theatre and made some sturdy brackets to hold it up, you can use cardboard and sticks to make a cast of characters for your show.

Take your time drawing the intricate theatre design, or simplify it if you want to.

Difficulty level: Easy

YOU WILL NEED

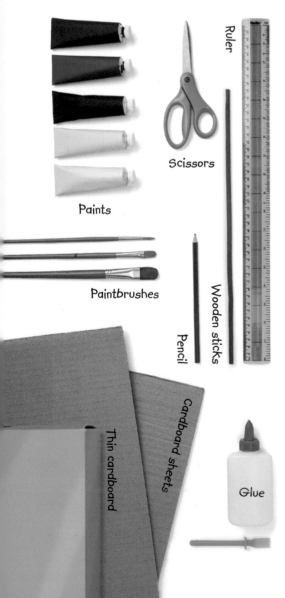

Paints

Scissors

Ruler

Paintbrushes

Pencil

Wooden sticks

Thin cardboard

Cardboard sheets

Glue

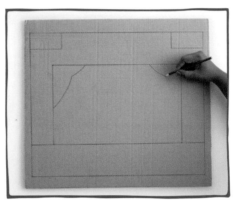

1 On a piece of cardboard, draw a large rectangle for your **stage**. Then copy the stage outline shown above.

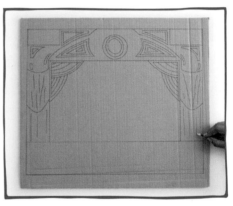

2 Now draw patterns around the stage. Work outwards, and try to make your design look the same on each side.

Follow the shape of the curtains.

3 Cut out a space in the centre. Don't forget to follow the shape of your curtains.

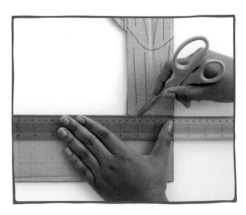

4 Score the horizontal line along the bottom of the rectangle so you can fold up the stage **floor**.

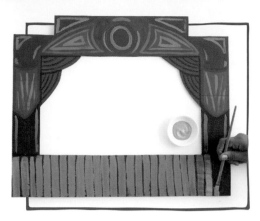

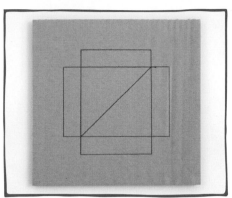

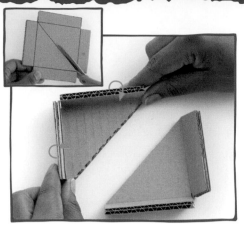

5 Now decorate your stage. Paint the floor orange and add brown lines to create a wooden effect.

6 Make **brackets** to hold up the stage. Draw a square and divide it in half with a diagonal line. Add tabs to each side.

7 Cut the shape out and cut along the diagonal line to create two brackets. Score and fold the tabs.

8 Paint the brackets in colours that match the stage. Make one tab the same colour as the stage floor.

9 Now fold up the stage floor. Glue your brackets to each side of the stage, fixing the orange tabs to the floor.

10 Draw any **characters** you like on card (or use pictures from magazines), paint them, and tape a wooden stick to the back of them.

Bring characters to life with fun stories.

11 Place your theatre on a surface that you can sit below, so you are out of view. If the theatre falls over, secure it with sticky tack. Hold the sticks to move your characters around the stage.

LAZY LIZARDS

There are more than 6,000 species of lizard on Earth and they come in all shapes, colours, and sizes. How about adding to nature's enormous collection by making your very own species? This is your chance to challenge your creativity and make the most eye-catching lizard in the world!

Add spines or a crest to make your lizard look more exotic.

Your lizard's tail can be any shape.

Even simple decorations look great if you use bold colours.

Add glitter to make your lizard stand out.

An egg box provides a ready-made cone shape for the lizard's head.

HOW TO MAKE
LAZY LIZARDS

These laid-back reptiles are quick and easy to make. You could make several eye-catching lizards and decorate them all differently, so that each one is unique and characterful.

Quick and easy to make, but **be as creative as you want** with the decoration.

Difficulty level: Easy

YOU WILL NEED

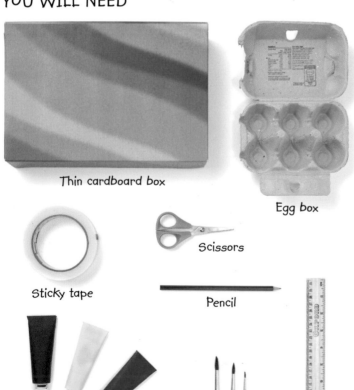

Thin cardboard box

Egg box

Sticky tape

Scissors

Pencil

Paints

Paintbrushes

Ruler

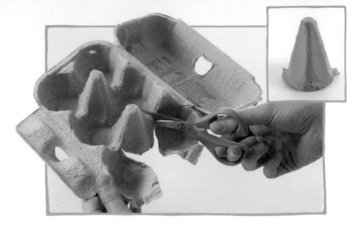

1 First make the **lizard's head**. Cut a cone out of the egg box by cutting around the base of one of the central divides.

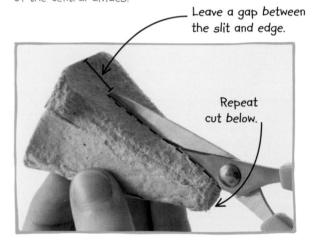

Leave a gap between the slit and edge.

Repeat cut below.

2 To add the **mouth**, cut a slit through the point of the cone on both sides. Don't cut all the way to the edge. Then, gently pull the slits apart.

3 Now make the lizard's **body**. Draw a rectangle on a piece of card from your box, using a ruler to keep the lines straight. Cut the rectangle out.

Fix tape to the
edge before you
begin rolling.

4 Roll the rectangle into a tube. Check it is wide
enough to fit snugly into the hollow end of the
head. Then tape the edge of the tube to secure it.

5 Push the body firmly into the head section.
Fix it in place by sticking strips of sticky tape
where the head and body join, on either side.

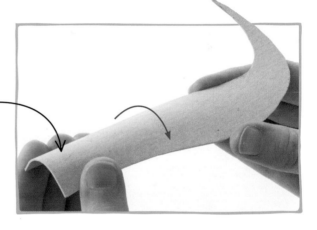

Bend the edge
of the tail gently
to curve it.

6 Now take another thin piece of card and draw
and cut out the lizard's **tail**. Your tail can be
curly, straight, wiggly, or even a zig-zag shape!

7 Bend the end of the tail to give it a slight
curve across its width. This will make it easier
to attach to the lizard's body.

8 Tape the tail to the body.
Use strips of sticky tape
on top and underneath the tail
to hold it securely in place.

Fix tape to the tube
before attaching the tail.

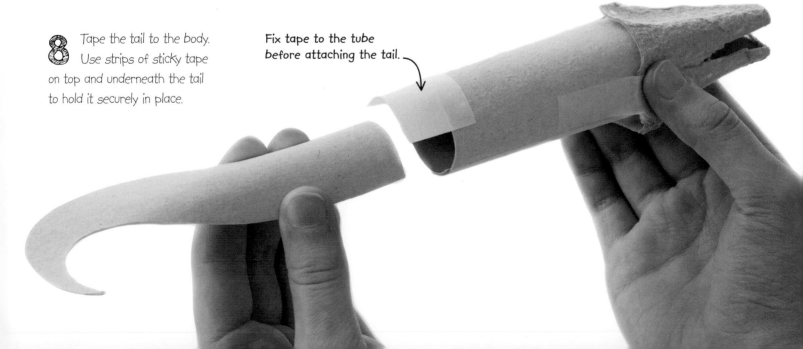

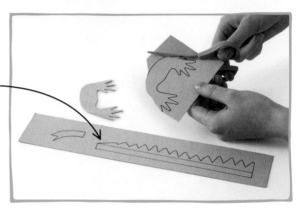

Make the spikes the same length as the body and tail.

9 Lay the lizard on another piece of thin card to see how big its **front legs** need to be. Draw the legs as a single piece. Repeat for the **back legs**.

10 Draw the lizard's **tongue** and **spikes** on a new piece of thin card. Add a tab to the spikes. Then cut out all the body parts.

Add notches if your lizard's tail is curved so you can bend the spikes.

11 Flip the lizard over and attach the legs to the body with sticky tape. Make sure the toes are facing in the right direction.

12 Attach the spikes to the lizard's back. Fold the tab along the spikes first, to make the spikes stand upright. Then, starting at the tail end, tape the tab along the lizard's body and tail.

Add scales in a lighter or darker shade.

Add a tongue.

Paint the features a different colour from the rest of the body.

13 Your lizard is now ready to decorate. Paint it in bright colours and patterns. Don't forget to add the eyes.

NOW TRY THIS

If you've made several lizards, you probably need a place to put them on show. People who own real reptiles often keep them indoors in a special tank called a vivarium. Why not use a cardboard box to build a vivarium for your lizards? You could even decorate it with exotic plants, which you can make by following steps 3–8 of the Tropical Aquarium project on pages 70–71.

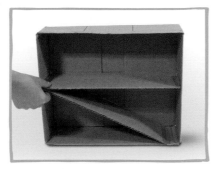

1 Take a medium-sized, shallow cardboard box and cut off the flaps. Do not discard them.

2 Position the flaps inside so they form a shelf and a ramp. Tape them securely in place.

3 Paint the inside of the box. Once the paint dries, your vivarium is ready for your lizards to move in.

Paint the ramp and shelf in a dark colour to make the lizards stand out.

Arrange the plants and lizards until you are happy with the display.

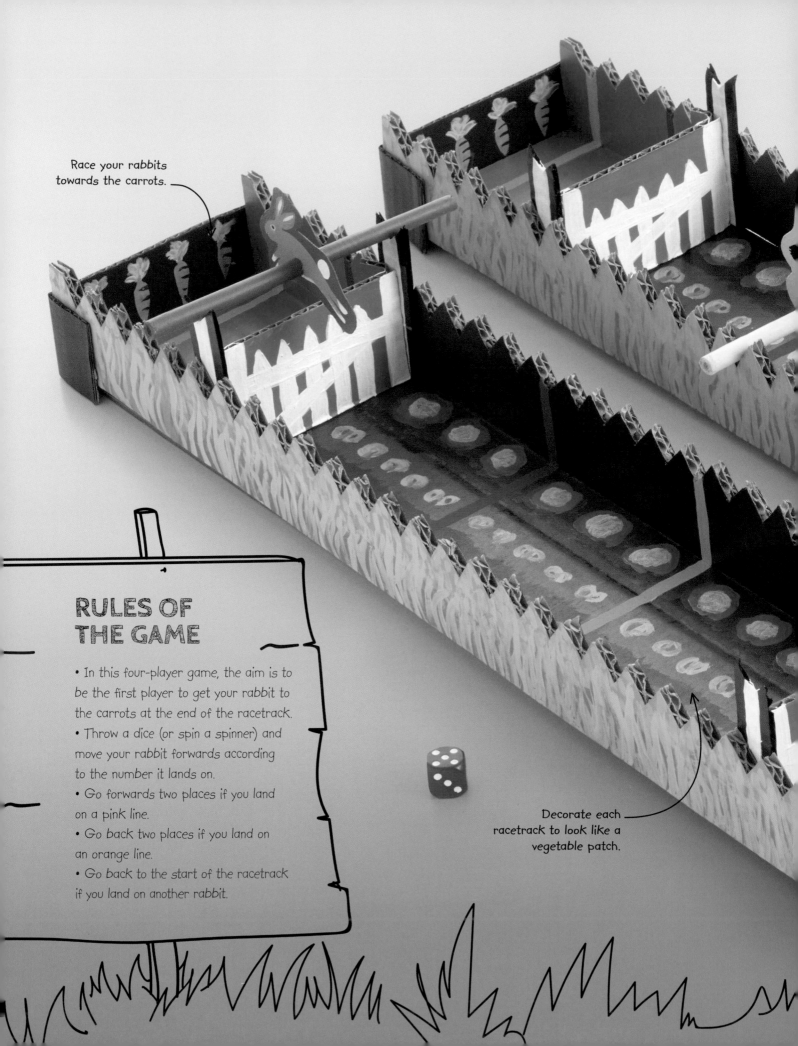

Race your rabbits towards the carrots.

Decorate each racetrack to look like a vegetable patch.

RULES OF THE GAME

• In this four-player game, the aim is to be the first player to get your rabbit to the carrots at the end of the racetrack.

• Throw a dice (or spin a spinner) and move your rabbit forwards according to the number it lands on.

• Go forwards two places if you land on a pink line.

• Go back two places if you land on an orange line.

• Go back to the start of the racetrack if you land on another rabbit.

Paper tubes support the rabbits on the racetrack.

RACING RABBITS

You'll love playing this thrilling rabbit race game! Make two vegetable patches with high fences for the rabbits to jump over. Then challenge your friends to see whose rabbit can get to the tasty carrots first.

Add fences to the racetracks.

This is the start of your racetrack.

HOW TO MAKE
RACING RABBITS

The first thing you'll need to make for this game is two identical cardboard racetracks. Measure both racetracks carefully so nobody has an unfair advantage when you play the game. Then use the template to make rabbits to race along the tracks.

Take your time to make sure everything is the right size and fits together.

Difficulty level: Medium

YOU WILL NEED

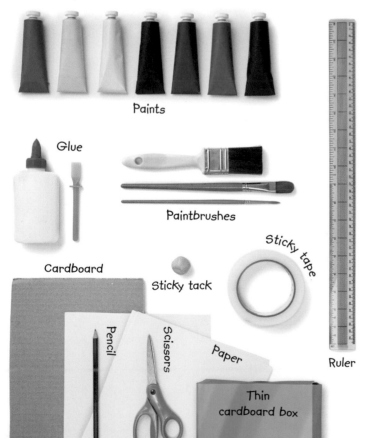

Paints

Glue

Paintbrushes

Cardboard

Sticky tack

Sticky tape

Pencil

Scissors

Paper

Thin cardboard box

Ruler

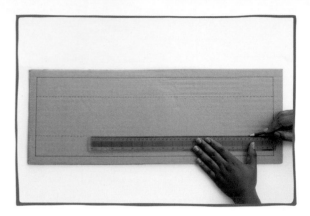

1 To make the **first racetrack**, draw a 20 × 60 cm (8 × 24 in) rectangle on cardboard. Add dotted lines 5 cm (2 in) in from the long edges.

Fold upwards to make the sides of the racetrack.

2 Cut the rectangle out. Score along the dotted lines and fold the sides upwards.

Flatten the rectangle again before marking the edges.

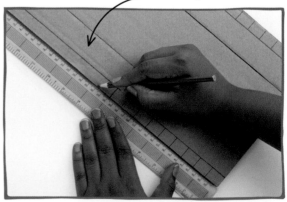

3 Draw a line 1 cm (½ in) in from one long edge of the rectangle. Then draw lines 2 cm (1 in) apart to divide the edge into equally spaced sections. Repeat the process on the other side.

4 Use a ruler to draw a symmetrical triangle inside each of the smaller sections that you have drawn along the edges of the racetrack.

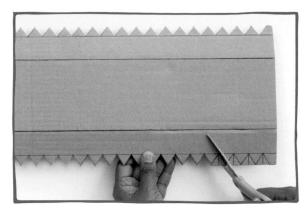

5 Cut out around the triangles to leave a zigzag edge. This will hold your rabbits in place. **Repeat steps 1–5** to make the **second racetrack**.

Paint on the details with a fine paintbrush.

6 Paint the racetracks and leave them to dry. Add pink and orange lines that reach from one side to the other.

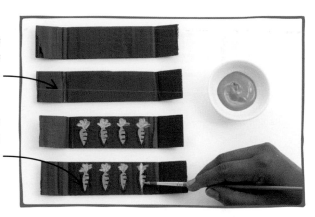

Fold up the ends of the brackets to make tabs.

Paint carrots for the winning rabbit.

7 To make the **start** and **end brackets**, cut out four strips of card that are about 5 cm (2 in) wider than the racetracks. Paint them brown, with carrot details on the two end brackets.

8 Fold the sides of the racetracks back up. Then glue the tabs on the brackets to the ends of each racetrack.

Your finished racetracks should be identical.

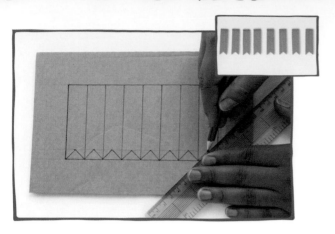

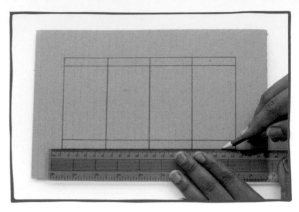

9 To make the **fenceposts**, draw a 7 x 20 cm (3 x 8 in) rectangle and divide it into eight equal sections. Mark a triangle on each post to match the notches on the racetrack and cut the fenceposts out.

10 Now make the **fences**. Draw four 6 x 9 cm (2½ x 3½ in) rectangles with 1 cm (½ in) tabs at either end.

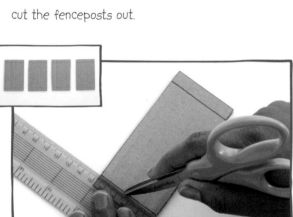

11 Cut all four rectangles out, then score along the tabs and fold them up.

12 Paint your fences green, then add the fence details in white. Paint the fenceposts black and white.

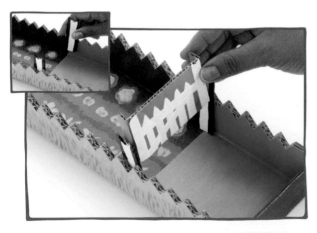

Copy the circle for the hole from the rabbit templates.

13 Glue the fenceposts to the edge of the racetrack. Then glue the tabs of the fences to the fenceposts. Each racetrack should have two fences with a post on each side of the fence.

14 Now use the rabbit templates (page 135) to draw four **rabbits** on card. Cut them out and paint them. Then pierce a hole in each rabbit using a pencil tip and carefully cut it out.

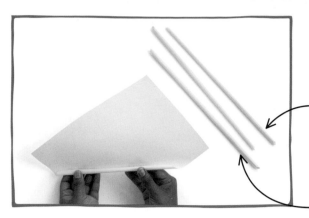

Make the tubes wide enough to fit snugly through the holes in the rabbits.

The tubes must be slightly longer than the width of the racetrack.

15 Roll four sheets of paper tightly into tubes and secure the edges with sticky tape. These will support your rabbits on the racetracks.

16 Paint the tubes in colours that match the backgrounds of your rabbit pieces. Then leave the paint to dry.

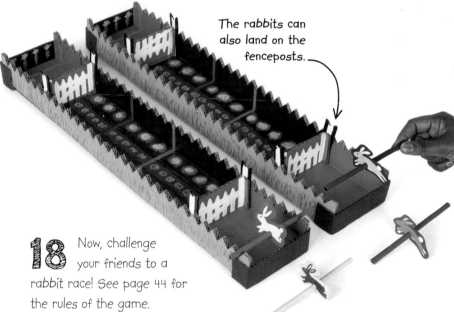

The rabbits can also land on the fenceposts.

17 Push and twist the tubes through the holes in the rabbits. Rest the rabbits on the notches of the racetracks, and trim the ends of the tubes if they are too long.

18 Now, challenge your friends to a rabbit race! See page 44 for the rules of the game.

NOW TRY THIS

If you prefer more exotic animals, why not make a kangaroo-themed racing game? You can also make a spinner to use instead of dice.

Use the kangaroo template (page 135).

Use the spinner template (page 135)

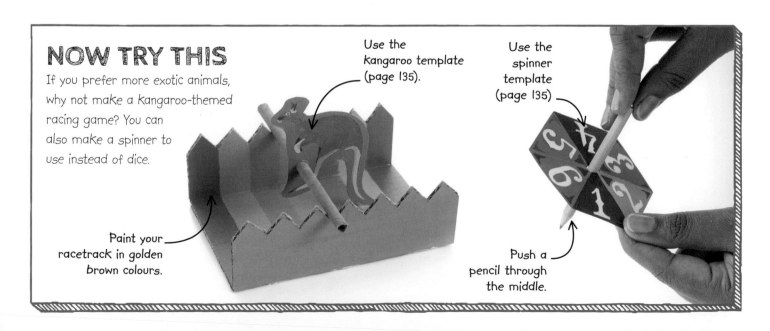

Paint your racetrack in golden brown colours.

Push a pencil through the middle.

PUPPET DRAGON

Dragons have appeared in myths and legends around the world for thousands of years. Now you can bring a flying dragon to life! Make it roar and snap its jaws with just a flick of your fingers.

HOW TO MAKE A
PUPPET DRAGON

This hand puppet uses six different templates, so make sure you will have enough card. Remember that you will need two big wings so that your dragon can fly!

Turn to pages 136–137 to **check the templates** before you start.

Difficulty level:
Medium

YOU WILL NEED

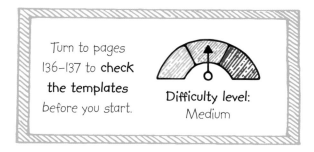

Paints

Scissors

Pencil

Paintbrushes

Glue

Thin cardboard box

Sticky tape

Cardboard sheets

1 Make the puppet's **upper jaw** first. Cut out a cardboard rectangle that's a little larger than your hand.

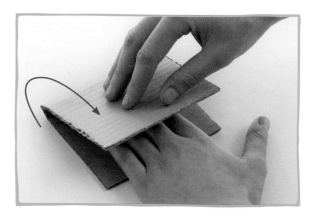

2 Fold the piece in the middle. Slide your fingers into the folded card to check that they fit.

3 Tape both sides of the jaw piece together, making sure that you have enough room for your fingers.

4 Repeat **steps 1–3** with a rectangle that is the same length, but half as wide. This will be the **lower jaw**, which will fit over your thumb.

Make sure the openings are in the middle.

5 To connect the jaws, cut out a strip of thin card that is narrower than the lower jaw. Tape it to both jaw pieces.

6 Fold the jaw so that the connecting strip of card is in the middle. Try the completed jaw on, with your thumb inside the lower jaw.

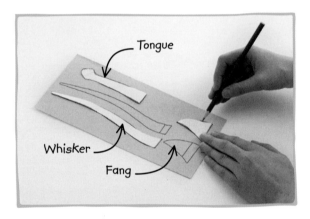

Tongue

Whisker

Fang

7 Copy the **whisker, tongue,** and **fang** templates (including tabs, where necessary) from pages 136–137 onto a piece of card. You will need a pair of whiskers and two fangs.

8 Cut out the five pieces. Then, add tabs to the fangs and whiskers (but not the tongue) by folding each piece along the line at the base.

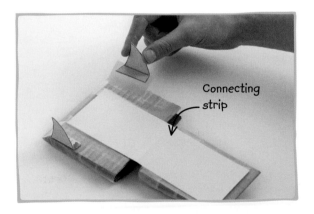

Connecting strip

9 Lay the jaw section flat with the connecting strip facing up, and attach the fangs by taping their tabs to either side of the upper jaw.

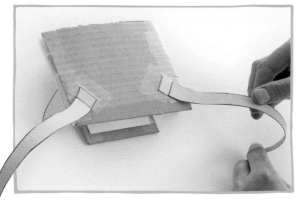

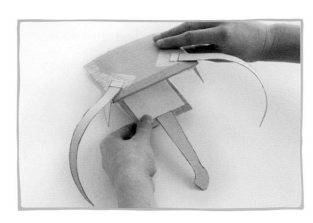

10 Flip the jaw section over and tape the tabs of the whiskers to the front corners of the upper jaw. Bend the whiskers into curves.

11 To complete the puppet's mouth, tape the straight edge of the tongue centrally to the front of the lower jaw, so the tip sticks out.

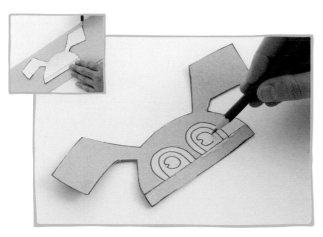

13 Tape the tab of the head section to the back of the dragon's upper jaw. Your puppet's head is now complete!

12 Copy the **head** template from page 136 onto some card and cut it out. Fold along the base line to create a tab. Draw eyes above the tab.

Tape the head so that it sits at the back of the jaw.

The whiskers should curl out.

You can curl the tongue piece if you like.

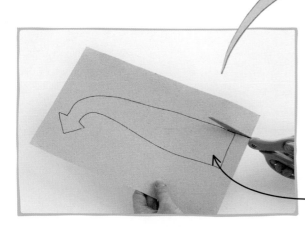

The neck should be narrower than the width of the lower jaw.

14 Copy the **body and tail** template from page 137 onto some card and cut it out.

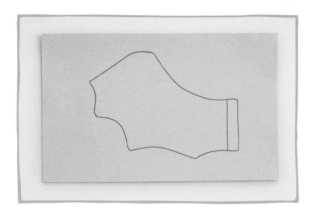

15 Copy the **wing** template from page 136 onto a piece of card and then cut it out.

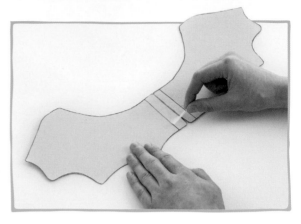

16 Repeat **step 15** for the second wing, and flip it over so you have a symmetrical pair of wings. Tape them together as shown.

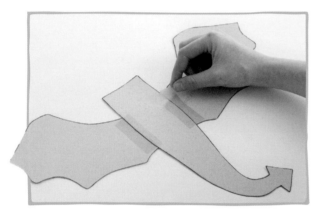

17 Tape the body section you made in **step 14** centrally across the wings, as shown. Turn it over and tape the other side if it doesn't feel secure.

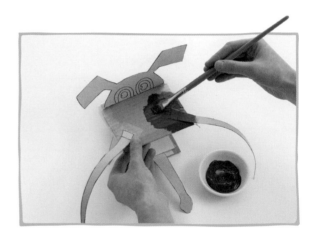

18 It's time to paint your puppet. Start with the head section. Paint it in a base colour first, leave it to dry, then paint the details on.

19 While the head section dries, decorate the puppet's body on both sides. Use bright colours to make your dragon bold and impressive. Let all the paint on the body section dry.

20 It's time to attach the body to the head. Dab glue along the edge of the neck.

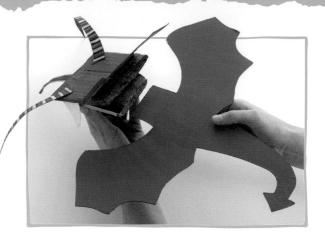

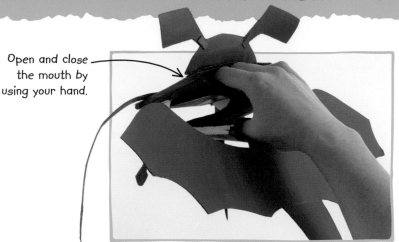

Open and close the mouth by using your hand.

21 Flip the *body* over and stick the *neck* to the underside of the *lower jaw*. Let the glue dry.

22 Now you can try your puppet on properly. Put your hand inside as shown, with the body hanging in front of your arm.

NOW TRY THIS

Now that you know how to make a puppet dragon, you can create other equally fabulous creatures with only a few changes. **Repeat steps 1–3** from the dragon, then make the alterations described below.

PUPPET FROG

Attach two small semi-circles for the eyes.

Make the two jaw pieces the same width.

Give the frog's feet long webbed toes.

Make a rectangle for the body and curved banana shapes for the legs.

Attach the feet and legs to a body rectangle.

PUPPET BIRD

Cut out a wide semi-circle shape for the head.

The jaw pieces can be shaped into a pointy beak.

Make feathery wings instead of scaly ones.

The toes on the bird should be shorter than the frog's.

HERO'S HELMET

No knight would be ready for battle without a helmet. Make your own protective headgear, complete with a visor, faceguard, and feather plume. Or, if knights are too old-fashioned, whip up a superhero mask or racing-driver's helmet.

HOW TO MAKE A
HERO'S HELMET

This Knight's helmet looks impressive but it's not hard to make. You can either ask someone to help you build it around your head, or make a balloon stand (see page 12) to give you a sturdy structure to work around. If you want to be certain that it will fit, you can measure each strip of card against your head before you cut it.

Make sure the balloon stand is **the right size**. You want a helmet that fits!

Difficulty level:
Medium

YOU WILL NEED

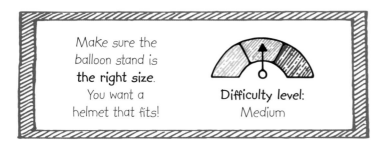

Paints

Strong tape

Paintbrushes

Scissors

Pencil

Cardboard sheets

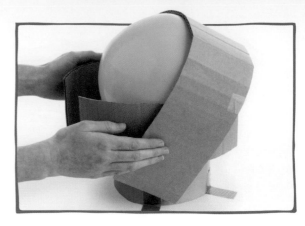

1 To make the **frame**, cut out two long strips of cardboard. Wrap one horizontally around your balloon stand at mouth height. Bend the other strip over the top, angling it towards the back slightly.

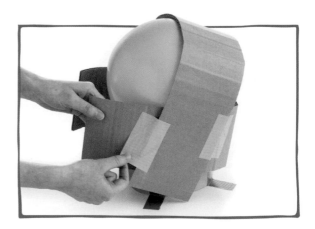

2 Stick the two strips together on either side of the join, using strong tape. Repeat on the other side.

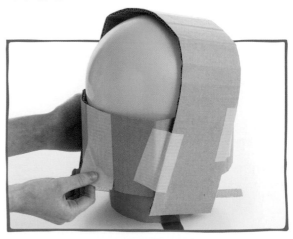

3 Now bring the ends of the horizontal strip together, at the front of the balloon stand. Overlap the edges slightly and tape them together.

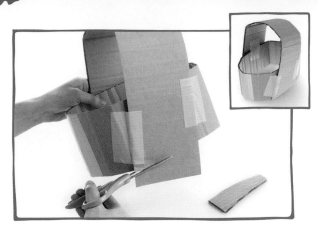

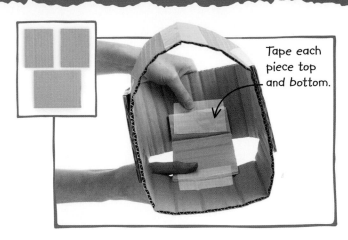

Tape each piece top and bottom.

4 Trim the ends off the vertical strip, so they are level with the horizontal strip. Add extra tape on the inside to strengthen the joins.

5 To fill in the hole at the back of the helmet, cut out three cardboard rectangles. Position one of your rectangles centrally and secure it with strong tape.

6 Tape the other two rectangles on either side of the piece you attached in **step 5**, to cover the gaps.

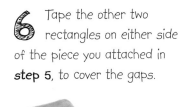

Bend the pieces to the curve of the helmet.

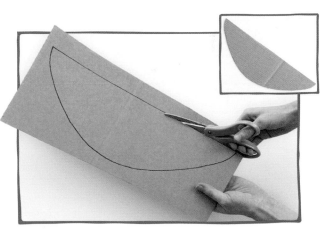

7 To make the **visor**, draw a stretched semi-circle shape on a piece of cardboard and then cut the shape out.

Tape the visor in an "open" position so that it won't cover your eyes.

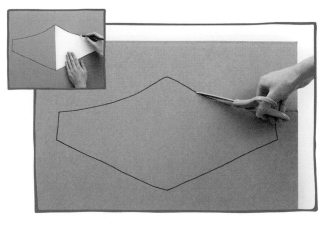

8 Bend the visor into a curved shape and tape the ends to either side of your helmet. Tape it on the inside too, to strengthen.

9 Use the template on page 138 to draw half of the **faceguard** on a piece of cardboard. Flip the template to draw the other half, then cut it out.

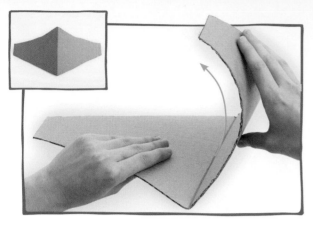

10 Fold the faceguard in half from point to point, then *bend* it into a curved shape on either side of the fold.

11 With the folded edge pointing outwards, attach the ends of the faceguard to either side of the helmet, using strong tape.

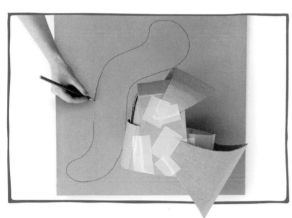

12 Now make the **plume**. Lay your helmet on its side on a piece of cardboard and use it as a guide to draw the plume. Then cut the shape out.

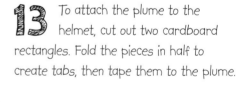

Make two tabs the same size.

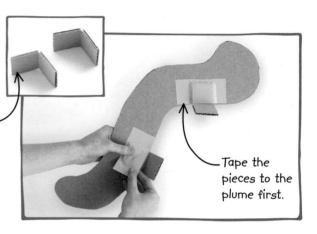

Tape the pieces to the plume first.

13 To attach the plume to the helmet, cut out two cardboard rectangles. Fold the pieces in half to create tabs, then tape them to the plume.

14 Position the plume against the *back* of the helmet and tape the tabs down.

15 Your Knight's helmet is now ready to decorate. Use grey or silver paint to create a metal effect. Paint the plume in any colour you want.

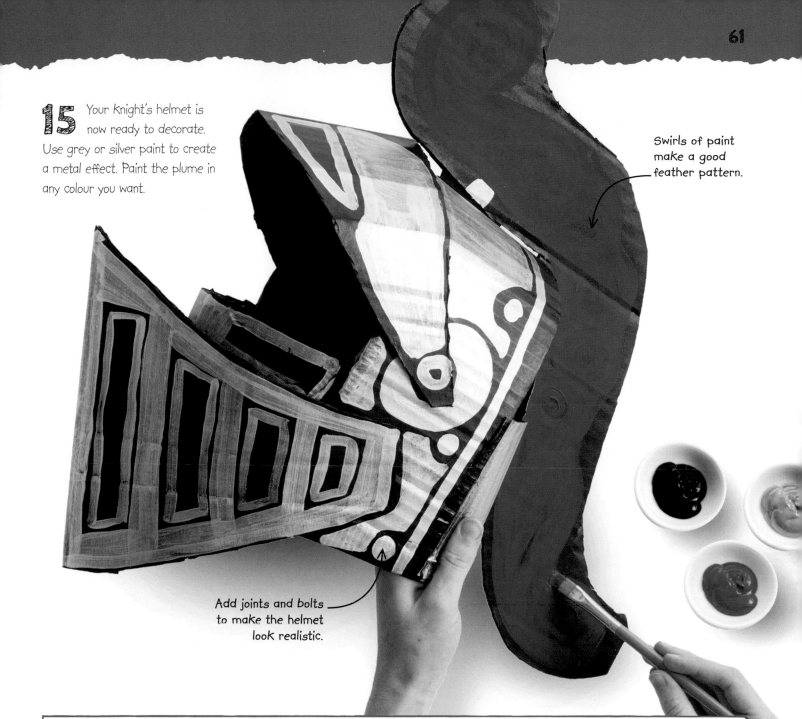

Swirls of paint make a good feather pattern.

Add joints and bolts to make the helmet look realistic.

NOW TRY THIS

You can use the *basic frame* of the knight's helmet to make other types of headgear. How about a crash helmet to go with the racing car on page 108, or a superhero's mask? Simply repeat **steps 1–6** to create the frame and then add different features.

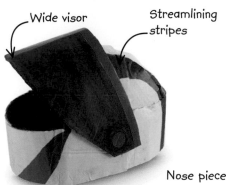

Wide visor

Streamlining stripes

To make a **racing-driver's helmet**, make a wide visor which covers more of your face. Then you are ready to race!

V-shaped visor

Nose piece

For a **superhero's mask**, make the visor a V-shape and position it lower. Cut out a gap for your mouth and add a nose piece.

Bottle tops and buttons make great robot features.

BOX ROBOTS

Would you like to travel through time to the distant future? Now you can, by transforming yourself into an incredible sci-fi robot! You'll need cardboard boxes that you can wear on your head, body, and hands. Then bring your box robot to life with mechanical designs.

Paint high-tech designs onto all parts of your box robot.

HOW TO MAKE
BOX ROBOTS

To make this fantastic robot costume, you'll need a big box for the robot's body, a square box for its head, and two smaller boxes for its hands. Make sure the boxes are big enough for you to wear. You'll be using cardboard circles and cups to add the robot's ears and eyes.

Take your time when you cut holes in the boxes for **a perfect fit**.

Difficulty level:
Medium

YOU WILL NEED

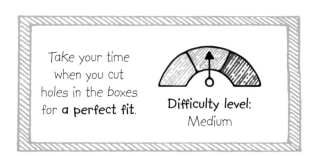

Paper cups

Large plate

Scissors

Ruler   Strong tape   Pencil   Paintbrushes

Paints

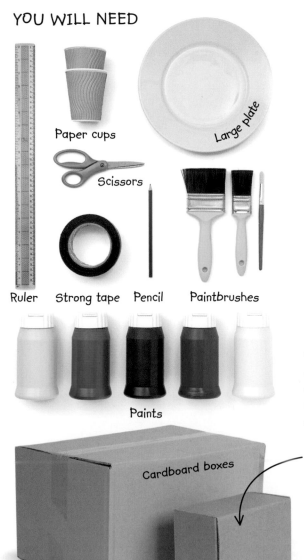

Cardboard boxes

You'll need cardboard sheets, a large box for the body, a smaller square box for the head, and two small boxes for the hands.

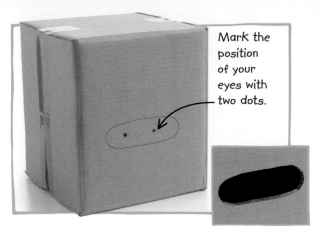

Mark the position of your eyes with two dots.

1 Place the square box over your head and mark the position of your eyes. Then remove the box and draw around the dots. Cut this shape out to make a slot for you to see through.

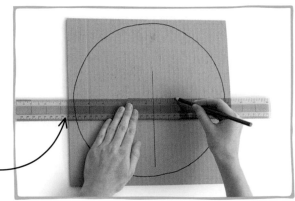

Use a ruler to draw your cross.

2 To create the **ears**, trace around a large plate on a piece of card. Mark the centre of the circle with a cross, then cut the circle out.

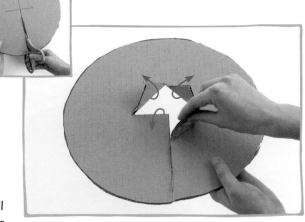

3 Cut along one arm of the cross from the outside of the circle to the centre. Cut short slits across the other arms of the cross and fold them upwards to make tabs.

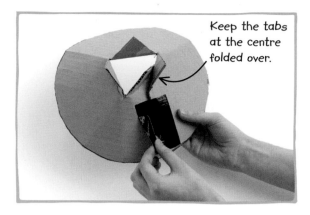

Keep the tabs at the centre folded over.

Fix the ears to the robot's head.

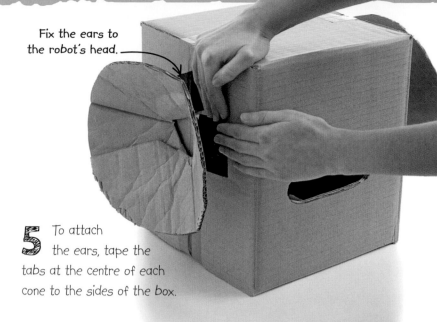

4 Pull the circle into a cone shape. Secure the overlapping edges of the cone with strong tape. **Repeat steps 2–4** to make a second ear.

5 To attach the ears, tape the tabs at the centre of each cone to the sides of the box.

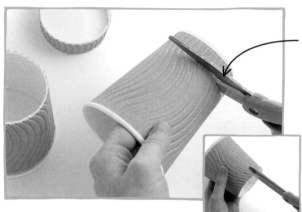

Cut slightly above the bottom of the cups.

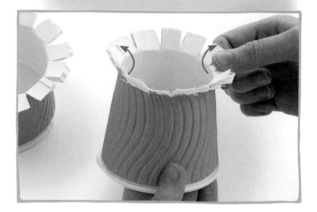

6 Now, make the **eyes**. Cut the base off two paper cups. Make slits around the bottom of each cup to create tabs.

7 Fold the tabs outwards so that you can easily stick the eyes to the robot's head.

8 Stick the eyes to the head by taping the tabs down.

Look at the position of the ears and attach the eyes at a similar height.

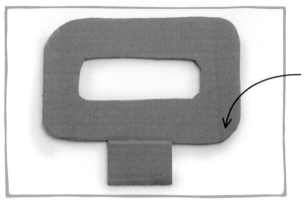

Your antenna can be any shape and size.

9 Draw an **antenna** shape on cardboard. You can use the picture above as a guide if you like. Cut the shape out.

10 Make a **support** for the robot antenna. Cut out a small rectangle with tabs on two of the sides as shown, and fold the tabs up.

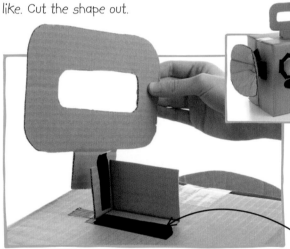

Make the shape wide enough to fit your head through.

Tape the longer flap to the head, and the antenna to the shorter flap.

11 Tape the support in place on top of the robot's head, then tape the antenna to the support.

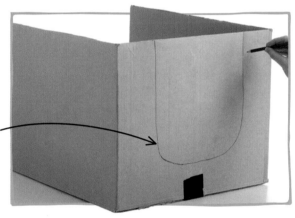

12 Now make the robot's **body**. Cut off one of the sides of the large box. Then draw a U shape on the opposite side and cut it out.

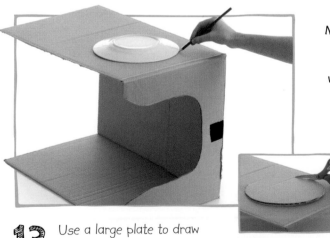

13 Use a large plate to draw circles on the other two sides of the box. Cut the circles out to make holes for your arms.

Make sure your pieces of cardboard are wider than your small boxes.

14 Next, make the robot's **hands**. Cut out two rectangular pieces of cardboard, roll them into tubes, and secure them with strong tape.

15 Take one of the small boxes and draw around the tube on each shorter side near the bottom. Then cut holes where you have drawn.

16 Push a tube through the two holes to make handles you can hold when you wear them. **Repeat steps 15 and 16** to make the other hand.

17 Finally, decorate each part of your robot. Paint a base coat first and let it dry. Then paint on futuristic designs in bright colours.

Make your decorations look like buttons, dials, screens, and switches.

Paint the head and ears in contrasting colours.

NOW TRY THIS

Why not make your robot even more high-tech by adding three-dimensional features to it? Try sticking on plastic lids, parts of egg boxes, and other cardboard shapes.

Egg box divides

Plastic lids

Give your robot big eyes using plastic lids.

TROPICAL AQUARIUM

Keeping an aquarium is a popular hobby for people around the world. Now you can make your own underwater scene, complete with colourful fish. All careful aquarists (people who keep aquariums) make sure their fish live in an environment similar to their natural habitats. So make a variety of coral, rocks, and underwater plants for your fish to hide between.

TROPICAL AQUARIUM

Turn your cardboard box into a beautiful aquarium with lots of coral features. Then, use the templates on page 139 to make a colourful array of tropical fish to display inside your aquatic world.

The **more features** you add to your aquarium, the more impressive it will look!

Difficulty level: Medium

YOU WILL NEED

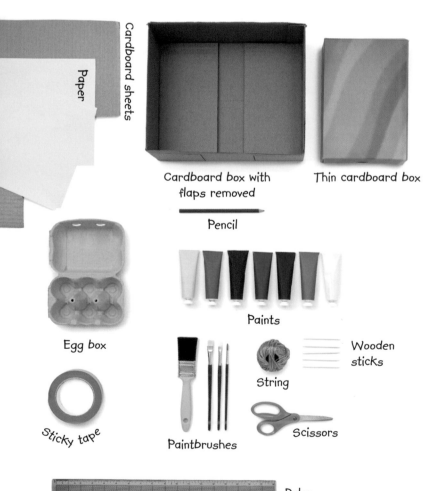

Paper

Cardboard sheets

Cardboard box with flaps removed

Thin cardboard box

Pencil

Egg box

Paints

Sticky tape

Paintbrushes

String

Wooden sticks

Scissors

Ruler

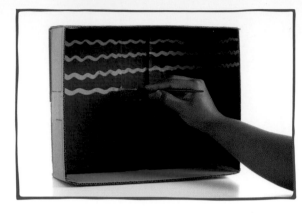

1 First make your **tank**. Paint the inside of your box dark blue. Paint the base in light blue and use the same colour to paint wavy lines for a watery effect.

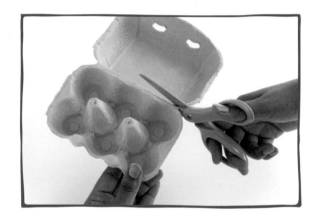

2 While the tank dries, make the various coral features. First, cut off the lid of your egg box to use as the **table coral**.

3 Carefully use your scissors to cut around the two central divides inside your egg box, to make **cone-shaped corals**.

4 To make an **ocean plant**, cut a rectangle out of thin card. Then cut wavy slits across it, leaving a 2 cm (1 in) edge for the base.

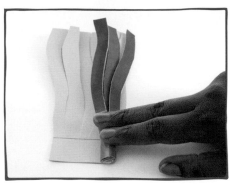

5 Roll up the piece of card tightly, starting from the base, so it forms a thin tube.

6 Then, hold the base so it remains rolled up, and wrap a piece of sticky tape around it to secure.

7 Bend the strips outwards to form the plant shape. Repeat **steps 4–7** to make plants of different shapes and sizes.

Hold and push the base on so you don't damage the plant.

8 Next, use a pencil to pierce the tops of your coral cones and push the base of a plant into each one.

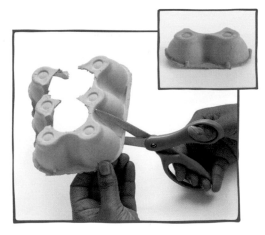

9 Now turn your egg box over and cut out the two remaining pieces at the end of your box, to make a double **dome-shaped coral**.

10 Take your double dome-shaped corals and pierce the tops in the same way as **step 8**. Push some more plants into the holes.

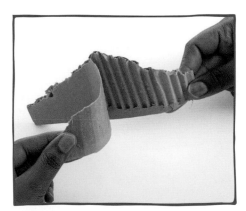

11 To make a **coral panel**, tear off a piece of corrugated cardboard. Carefully peel away the thin top layer to revel the bumpy texture underneath.

12 Use a ruler and scissors to score along the length of the panel, about 2 cm (1 in) from the base. Repeat **steps 11–12** to make more coral panels.

Use lighter colours to add detail to your plants.

Use contrasting colours to add detail and texture to your coral.

Corrugated card gives a nice texture to coral panels.

Paint your table coral all one colour.

Use paper to make rocks.

13 Paint your coral features in bright colours. Add **rocks** to your scene by scrunching up paper into balls and paint them, too.

14 Once your painted pieces are dry, add a strip of sticky tape along the base of your **coral panels**.

15 Then, stick them inside your aquarium. Place one on the bottom and stick another to the side.

16 Now, arrange the rest of your coral features and rocks inside the aquarium however you want.

17 To make **tropical fish**, use the templates on page 139 to draw fish on thin card, then cut them out.

18 Paint your collection of fish in bold colours and pretty patterns, adding eyes, mouths, and gills.

19 To add your beautiful fish to the aquarium, tape a piece of string to the back of a few of your fish.

20 Then, use a sharp pencil to carefully pierce holes at the top of your aquarium.

21 Feed each piece of string through a hole from the inside and secure it with a knot.

22 Finally, tape the remaining fish to wooden sticks and push the ends into the coral shelf and features to complete the scene.

Adjust the strings so that the fish are hanging at different heights.

Paint the wooden sticks blue so they match the ocean scene.

NOW TRY THIS

To add some movement to your underwater scene, carefully cut thin slots out of the sides of your aquarium. Then draw two of your favourite sea creatures on thin card. Cut them out and decorate them, then tape each one to a long wooden stick. Poke your new sea creatures through the slots of your aquarium, to create your own aquatic show!

Use painted wooden sticks to move your sea creatures.

Cut a narrow opening along each side of the aquarium.

PHARAOH'S FINERY

Make your own
Egyptian headdress,
fit for a pharaoh and
perfect for any fancy
dress occasion.

Scarab beetle
decoration

Add a collar to
make your outfit
even more
impressive.

HOW TO MAKE PHARAOH'S FINERY

You'll look fabulous in this dazzling Egyptian headdress! Take your time and decorate it however you want, but make sure you choose nice bright colours. It is important to measure each piece against your body and adjust the size to fit you, so you may want to ask someone to help.

Copy your templates really **carefully** for this project.

Difficulty level: Medium

YOU WILL NEED

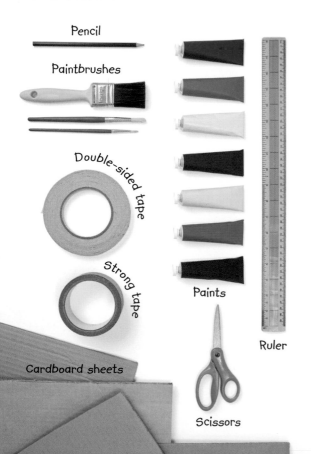

Pencil

Paintbrushes

Double-sided tape

Strong tape

Cardboard sheets

Paints

Ruler

Scissors

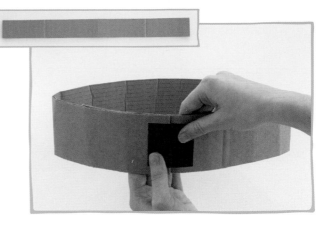

1 Cut a strip of cardboard and wrap it around your head for a snug fit. Trim off any excess, then tape the ends together to make a **headband.**

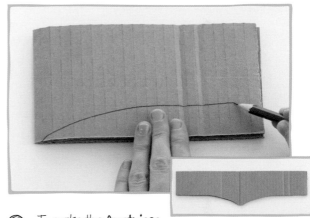

2 To make the **frontpiece,** cut a piece of cardboard that is slightly wider than the headband and half its length. Fold the piece in half, draw a curved line along the bottom, and cut along the line.

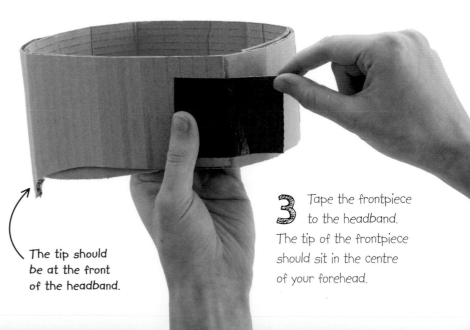

The tip should be at the front of the headband.

3 Tape the frontpiece to the headband. The tip of the frontpiece should sit in the centre of your forehead.

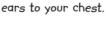

The braids should reach from your ears to your chest.

4 Next, make the **braids.** Cut out two identical rectangles of card, and use a ruler to draw straight lines across them. Cut along the lines, but don't cut all the way to the end.

5 Paint the braids a yellow base coat. Then add details to the tips in contrasting colours.

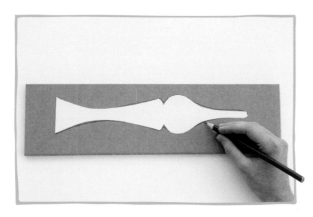

If you like, you can copy the details from the pendant template.

6 Now make the **pendants.** Use the pendant template on page 140 to draw two shapes on cardboard. Cut the pendant shapes out.

7 Paint a yellow base coat on the pendants and add details in contrasting colours once the paint has dried.

Tip of the frontpiece

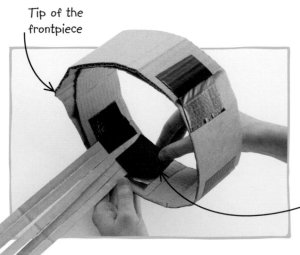

Tape the braids to the inside of the headband.

You can paint over the tape when you paint the headband.

8 Once the braids are dry, tape them to the inside of the headband on either side, so they will dangle over your ears.

9 Once the pendants are dry, use strong tape to attach them to the outside of the headband so they hang over the braids.

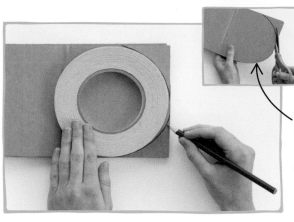

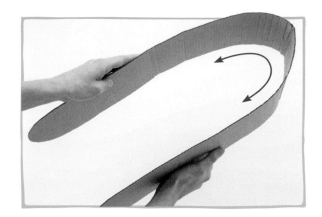

Cut along your markings to round the ends of the strip.

10 To make the **hood**, cut a strip of card long enough to reach from one collarbone to the other when curved over your head. Draw round a roll of tape at each end.

11 Bend the hood into a curved shape so that it will fit snugly over the top of your head when you attach it to the headband.

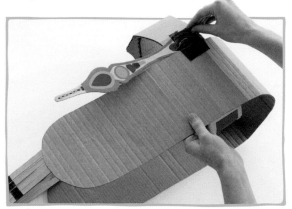

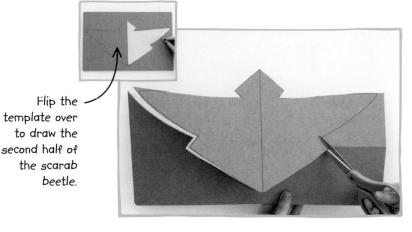

Flip the template over to draw the second half of the scarab beetle.

12 Use strong tape to secure the hood to the headband. Place the hood over the braids, but make sure it doesn't cover the pendants.

13 Next, use the scarab beetle template on page 140 to draw half of the **scarab beetle**. Flip it over to draw the other side, then cut the scarab out.

15 Carefully stick the scarab beetle to the top of the frontpiece. Its bottom point should line up with the tip.

Press down firmly at the front to fix the scarab beetle in place.

14 Draw scarab details onto the shape in pencil. You can copy the details from the template. Then put double-sided tape on the back of the shape, along the bottom.

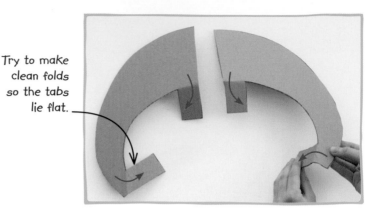

Try to make
clean folds
so the tabs
lie flat.

16 Use the template on page 141 to draw the first **crown piece** on cardboard. Flip the template to draw the second one. Cut both pieces out.

17 Fold the tabs on the crown pieces back on themselves, as shown above. This will help you secure the crown pieces to the hood.

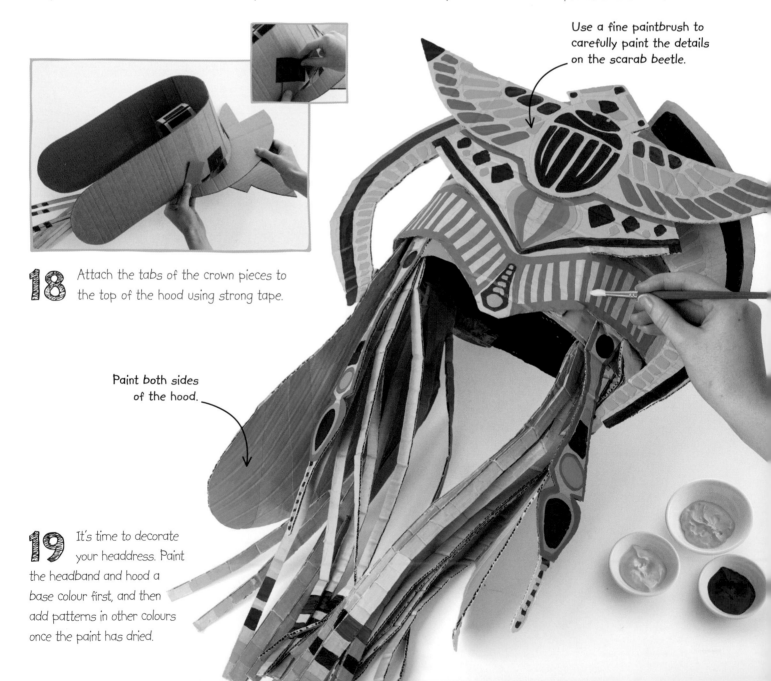

Use a fine paintbrush to carefully paint the details on the scarab beetle.

18 Attach the tabs of the crown pieces to the top of the hood using strong tape.

Paint both sides of the hood.

19 It's time to decorate your headdress. Paint the headband and hood a base colour first, and then add patterns in other colours once the paint has dried.

NOW TRY THIS

Make some matching accessories to complete your pharaoh outfit. For the **cuffs**, you will need two strips of cardboard long enough to wrap around your wrist, with some excess. For the **collar**, you will need a large piece of cardboard wider than your shoulders.

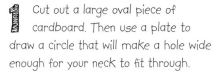

HOW TO MAKE CUFFS

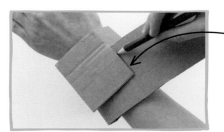

Mark where the cuff fits round your wrist.

1 Cut a slit near one end of your cardboard strip. Wrap the strip tightly around your wrist, and slot the other end through the slit.

Edges can be curved.

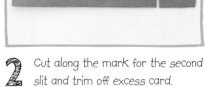

2 Cut along the mark for the second slit and trim off excess card. Now make a second cuff.

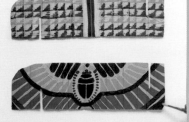

3 Paint the cuffs one colour and leave them to dry. Then draw details in pencil and paint them in contrasting colours to match the headdress.

HOW TO MAKE A COLLAR

1 Cut out a large oval piece of cardboard. Then use a plate to draw a circle that will make a hole wide enough for your neck to fit through.

2 Cut out the shape, with an opening between the inner circle and outer oval so that you can put the collar on.

3 Bend the front and back of the piece so the collar curves over your shoulders when you wear it.

4 Paint the piece all one colour and leave it to dry. Draw the details in pencil and paint them in striking colours.

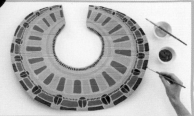

ADVENTURE CASTLE

Castles are the setting for all kinds of amazing stories. Your cardboard fortress can be home to knights and dragons, princes and princesses, or ghosts and vampires.

Populate your castle with different characters.

Short tower

Small tower

Add a flag with a pole made out of a cocktail stick.

Tall tower

Decorate the castle surroundings with trees to bring the scene to life.

Walkway

Castle entrance

Curtain wall

HOW TO MAKE AN
ADVENTURE CASTLE

The main part of the castle is made out of a large cardboard box. Keep the bits you cut off and use them to make the walkways and towers.

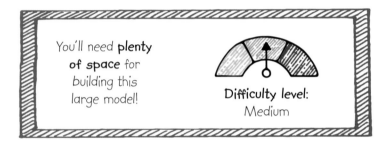

You'll need **plenty of space** for building this large model!

Difficulty level:
Medium

YOU WILL NEED

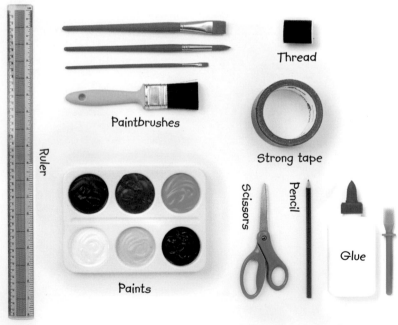

Ruler

Paintbrushes

Thread

Strong tape

Scissors

Pencil

Glue

Paints

Cardboard boxes

Cardboard sheets

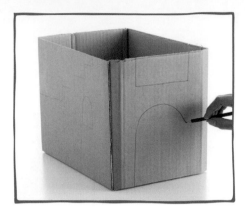

1 Make the **entrance** out of your large box. On the front, draw a rectangle for the roof and the drawbridge below.

2 Draw a stairway on one side. Extend the line from the lowest step across the back wall. Add a window below the stairs.

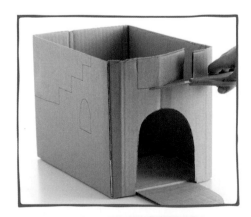

3 Cut out the drawbridge, leaving it attached at the base, and fold it out. Cut out the rectangular piece at the top.

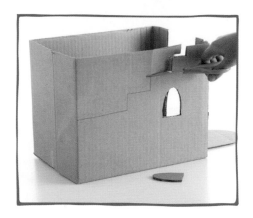

4 Carefully cut out the window and stairway. Keep the pieces that you cut out so you can trace around them.

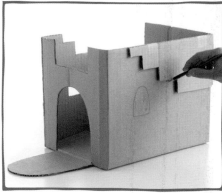

5 Trace around the pieces you cut in **step** 4 to draw a window and stairway on the other side of the box.

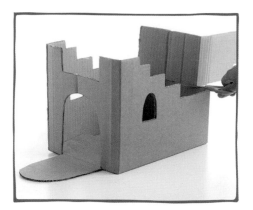

6 Cut out the window and stairway on the other side. Cut off the back wall along the line you marked in **step** 2.

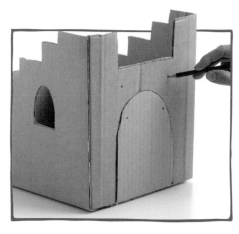

7 To complete the drawbridge, pierce two holes into the top of the drawbridge and two holes in the wall above.

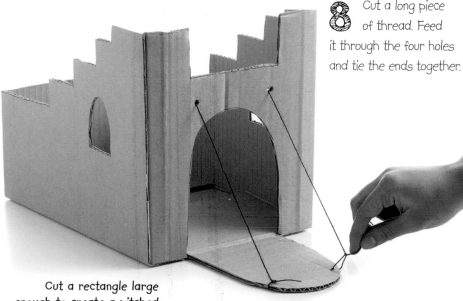

8 Cut a long piece of thread. Feed it through the four holes and tie the ends together.

Cut a rectangle large enough to create a pitched roof for your keep.

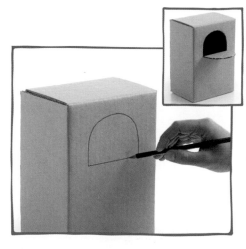

9 Make the **keep** out of your small box. Draw a window on the front. Cut it out, leaving it attached at the base, and fold it outwards.

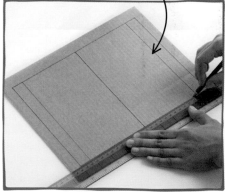

10 For the roof, draw a rectangle with a line through the centre and tab outlines at each end. Cut the roof out.

11 Fold the roof along the central line. Fold the tabs inwards and glue them to the top of the keep.

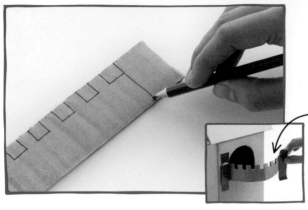

Battlements are the notches along the top of castle walls.

12 Draw **battlements** on a cardboard strip with tabs at either end. Cut the strip out, fold the tabs over, and tape the tabs to the keep so the strip fits around the window ledge.

13 Now make a **short tower**. Cut out a piece of cardboard 35 cm (14 in) long and as tall as the castle entrance. Roll it into a tube.

14 Bring the ends together so they overlap by 5 cm (2 in) and tape the edge down. Repeat **steps 13** and **14** to create another short tower.

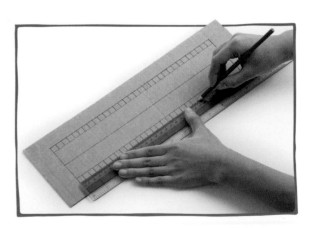

15 To add **flat roofs** to your short towers, draw around the towers on a piece of cardboard.

The end you draw around will become the top of the tower.

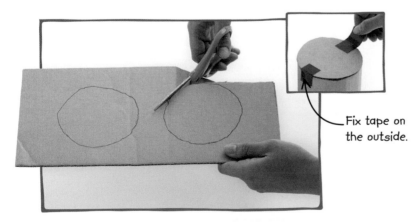

Fix tape on the outside.

16 Cut out the two circular shapes and tape them to the top of the towers. All that remains is adding battlements to the towers.

17 To make the battlements, draw a 30 cm x 8 cm (12 in x 3 in) rectangle. Add a line across the centre and a row of small squares along the edges.

18 Cut the piece along the horizontal line to make two identical pieces. Then, cut out every other square tab to complete the battlements.

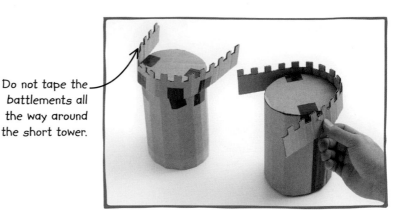

Do not tape the battlements all the way around the short tower.

19 Wrap a battlement strip around the top of each short tower. Tape the middle section to the tower and leave the ends loose.

20 For the **walkway**, cut out a 30 x 12 cm (12 x 5 in) cardboard piece. Cut battlements into the sides. Score and fold the piece 4 cm (1.5 in) from each edge.

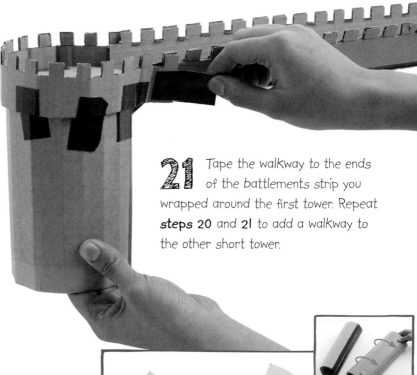

21 Tape the walkway to the ends of the battlements strip you wrapped around the first tower. Repeat **steps 20** and **21** to add a walkway to the other short tower.

Height of short tower.

22 Make a **tall tower** out of a 30 x 36 cm (12 x 14 in) cardboard piece. Draw the entrance, making its base level with the height of the short tower.

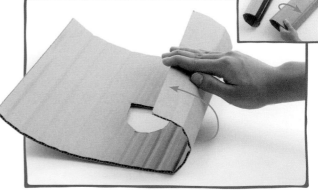

23 Cut out the entrance. Roll the piece into a tube and tape the overlapping ends together. Repeat **steps 22** and **23** to make another tall tower.

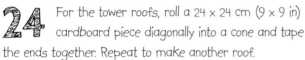

Add more tape to make the join stronger.

Push the roofs down onto the tall towers to the secure them in place.

24 For the tower roofs, roll a 24 x 24 cm (9 x 9 in) cardboard piece diagonally into a cone and tape the ends together. Repeat to make another roof.

25 Hold each cone by the pointy end and trim the *base* to make it level all the way round.

26 Place the cone roofs on top of your tall towers. You do not need to tape them to the towers, as they will stay in place when you push them down.

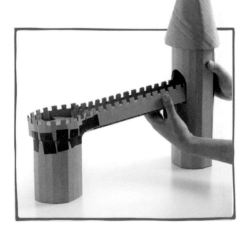

27 Link each short tower to a tall one by slotting the walkway into the tall tower entrance.

28 Make **small towers** out of cardboard pieces half the size of those used for the tall towers.

29 Repeat **steps 22–26** (without windows) to complete the **small towers**. They will flank the castle entrance.

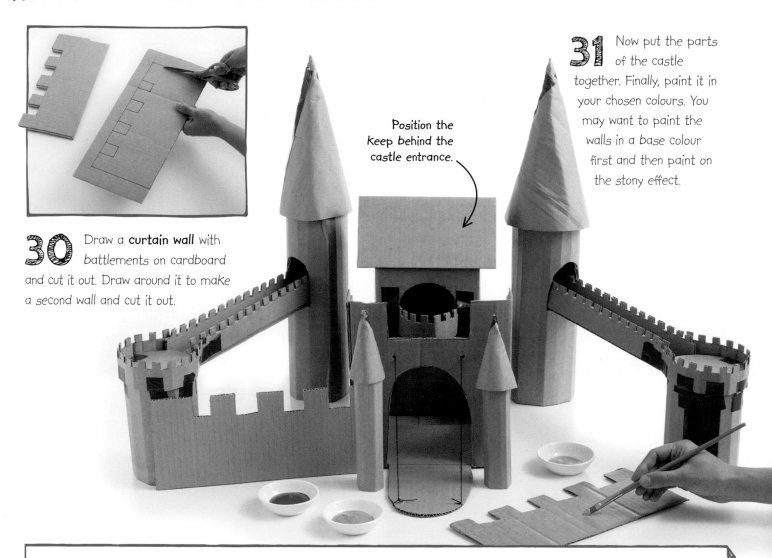

31 Now put the parts of the castle together. Finally, paint it in your chosen colours. You may want to paint the walls in a base colour first and then paint on the stony effect.

Position the keep behind the castle entrance.

30 Draw a **curtain wall** with battlements on cardboard and cut it out. Draw around it to make a second wall and cut it out.

NOW TRY THIS

Populate your castle with an array of characters. Draw the outline of your characters on cardboard (or use the templates on page 139), cut them out, and paint on the faces and bodies. To make a stand, cut two slits at the base of each character and push the ends of a folded strip of card into the slits.

The stand is made out of a folded strip of cardboard.

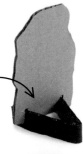

Your characters can be good, evil, magical, historical, or spooky. You decide!

PENGUIN FAMILY

If you've ever enjoyed watching penguins splashing around at the zoo, you'll love playing with these adorable creatures! All you need to make them is a sheet of card. Penguins are extremely sociable animals, so why not make an entire family of penguins to keep each other company?

HOW TO MAKE A
PENGUIN FAMILY

To make this family of friendly penguins, you'll need to follow the penguin template (page 142) very carefully. Don't cut the strips in your card too far, and make sure you always know which part of the penguin each strip will be.

Make sure you **slot your strips of card** into the right place.

Difficulty level:
Medium

YOU WILL NEED

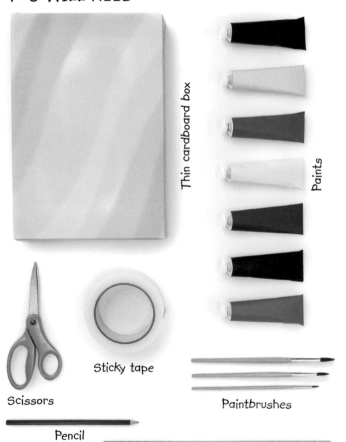

Thin cardboard box

Paints

Scissors

Sticky tape

Paintbrushes

Pencil

Ruler

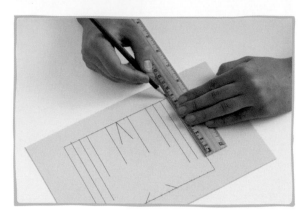

1 Cut out a large piece of thin card. Then copy the penguin template on page 142 onto your card. Use a ruler to keep your lines straight.

2 Cut slits along the lines. You should have seven strips to make various parts of the penguin, plus a thin strip at either end for the stand.

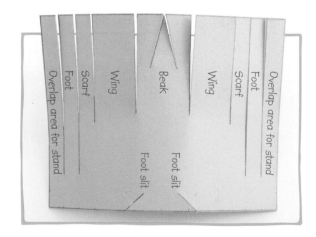

3 Carefully copy the words on the template to label each strip with the correct part of the penguin. Look at the picture above to help you.

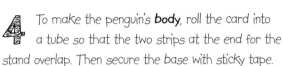

Tape along the inside of the tube to secure it.

4 To make the penguin's **body**, roll the card into a tube so that the two strips at the end for the stand overlap. Then secure the base with sticky tape.

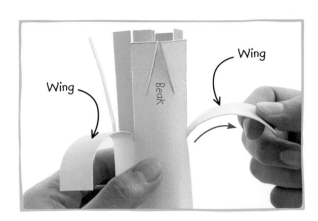

Wing

Wing

Beak

5 Make the penguin's **wings**. Gently bend the wing strips outwards to give your penguin a pair of flapping wings.

7 Look at your penguin in progress. Make sure you are clear which strip is which.

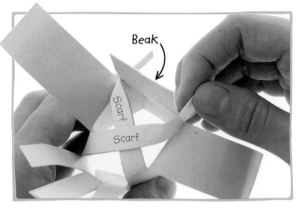

Beak

Scarf

Scarf

6 Create the **scarf** by bending the scarf strips inwards so they cross inside the tube. Slot the ends on either side of the beak strip at the front.

8 Bend the **beak** section back slightly and wrap the scarf strips around the base. Draw a short line where the strips meet in the middle, as shown.

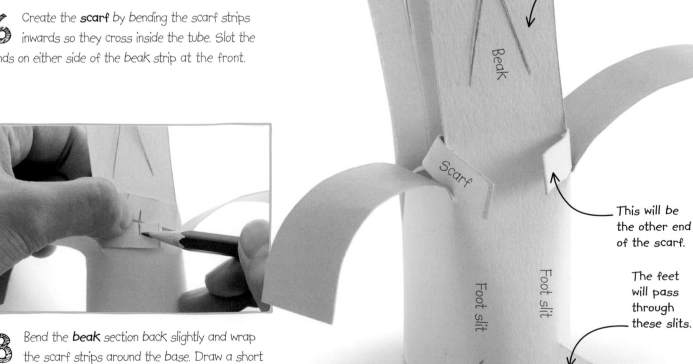

Beak

Scarf

Foot slit

Foot slit

This part will become the beak and face.

This will be the other end of the scarf.

The feet will pass through these slits.

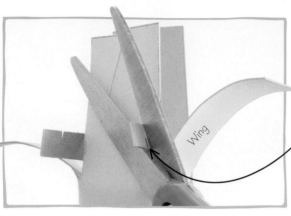

Lock the strips in place using the slits.

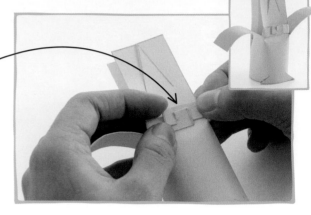

Wing

Don't cut any further than your pencil marks.

9 Cut slits along the pencil marks in the scarf strips. Make sure you don't cut all the way through the strips.

10 Pull the strips back into position and fasten them together by slotting the slits into one another to secure the scarf.

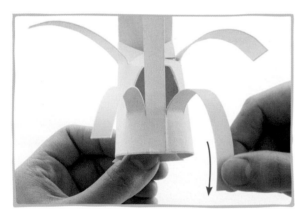

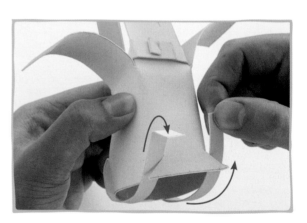

11 Now make the **feet**. Bend the two foot strips outwards and pull them *back* underneath the tube. Then turn your penguin around.

12 Bring the foot strips to the front of the penguin and slot them into the foot slits. Fold down the ends of the strips to create **toes**.

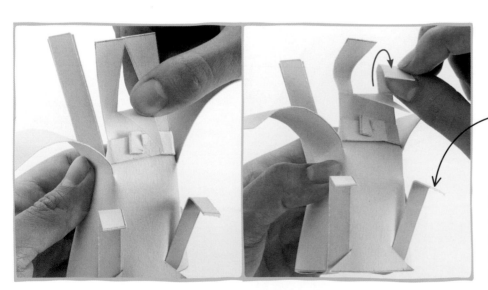

If the feet slide out of place, secure them from the inside with sticky tape.

13 Now make the penguin's **face**. Fold the V shape in the beak strip outwards to make the **beak**. Then, bend the tops of the two strips either side of the beak into curved **eye** shapes.

14 Finally, bend the remaining strip at the back of the penguin into an arc shape. You can use this strip to stand your penguin up.

15 Check that the strips are in the right place before you paint your penguin.

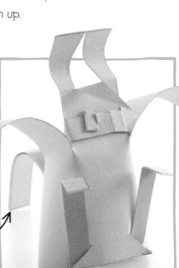

The strip at the back should prop your penguin up.

16 Now decorate your penguin. Use a fun, bright colour for the scarf.

Paint eyes on these flaps.

Paint the penguin's body black and white, and its beak and feet orange.

Paint both sides of each foot.

Make each tube the same colour as the penguin's scarf.

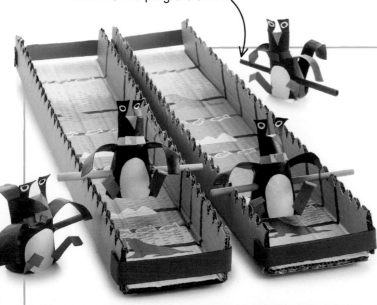

NOW TRY THIS

Turn your penguins into players for an icy-themed version of the game Racing Rabbits, featured on page 44. Follow the instructions on pages 46–48 to make the racecourses and paint them to look like icy streams. Use a sharp pencil to pierce a hole through the penguin's body just below the wings. Then push a coloured tube through the hole.

CARDVILLE CITY

Welcome to Cardville, a city where everything is made from recycling! By gathering up boxes and tubes of all sizes, you can create any town you like, from a classic country village to a futuristic metropolis.

You can add extra tubes and triangles to make your buildings more elaborate.

Stack up tubes and boxes to create impressive skyscrapers.

HOW TO BUILD
CARDVILLE CITY

Cardville works best with lots of buildings, so make as many as you can. The good news is that they don't all need to be the same. Your city will look more realistic if your buildings are slightly different shapes and sizes.

Find all kinds of **small boxes and tubes** around the house, or make your own.

Difficulty level: Hard

YOU WILL NEED

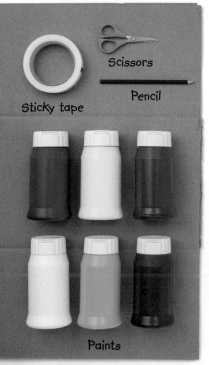

Thin cardboard box

Cardboard sheets

Sticky tape

Scissors

Pencil

Glue

Paints

Paintbrushes

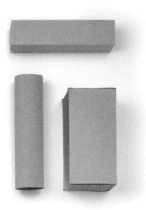

Small boxes and cardboard tubes

BUILDINGS

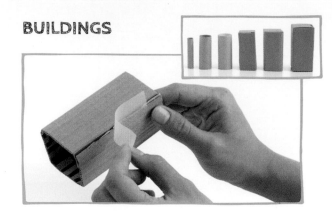

1 If you can't find any small boxes for your **buildings**, you can make your own. First, cut out a rectangle of thick card. Fold it as shown to form a rectangular tube and secure it with sticky tape.

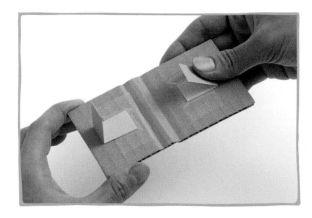

2 To make a **roof**, cut out a cardboard rectangle and fold it in half. Cut out two strips of thin card and tape each one to either side of the fold. Then fold each thin piece of card to create tabs.

3 To fix the roof in place, attach a piece of sticky tape to the end of each tab. Push each tab inside the tube and press the tape down against the walls.

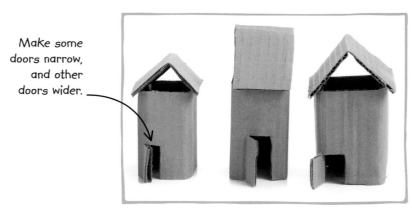

Make some doors narrow, and other doors wider.

4 Draw a **door** on the front of the building, then cut along one side and across the top. Fold the door outwards to open it.

5 Repeat steps 1-4 as many times as you like to create houses of different shapes and sizes.

If you've made your own box, tape card over the top.

6 Make **skyscrapers** by stacking up boxes and tubes of different sizes and fixing them together with glue or tape.

7 Paint your buildings in a range of colours, adding windows and any other details you like.

Try picking out roofs and doors with bright colours.

WALKWAY

Cut an X across the outline, then push the flaps into the box.

1 To make a **walkway**, take a long, thin box (or make your own box), line it up against the side of a building and draw around it. Cut across the outline and shape the flaps with your fingers to leave a neat hole.

2 Repeat the process with another similar building, then slot the ends of your walkway into the two holes. Tape in place if necessary.

CLOCK TOWER

Use a rectangle of thin card to make the roof.

1 To make a **clock tower**, tape a short, wide box to the top of a tall, thin box. Add a roof as you did for the other buildings.

2 Stick a cardboard circle to the front of the smaller box. Then decorate your clock.

CITYSCAPE

Score lines across the road so it folds down neatly.

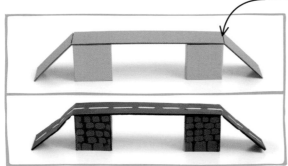

1 To build a **bridge**, take two small boxes and tape them to a strip of thick card. Decorate the card as a road and the boxes as brick walls.

2 To make a **garden hedge**, cut a strip of card and fold it into a large square as shown. Tape the ends of the strip together.

Use two different shades of green to give your plants a leafy texture.

3 To make **garden plants**, draw a variety of different trees and plants on a piece of thin card and cut them out.

4 Glue the plants to the hedge, then decorate them with green and brown paint. Sit a small house in the middle of your garden.

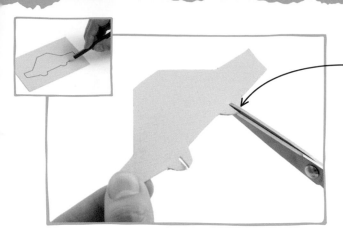

Cut slits in the middle of each wheel.

5 Draw a selection of different **cars** on thin card and cut them out. Use scissors to snip small slits in the car wheels.

6 Cut out small rectangles of card and snip short slits into them. Push them onto the wheels so that your cars can stand up.

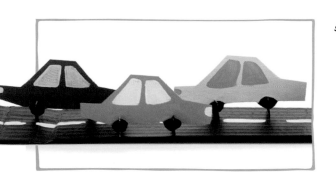

Use a ruler to draw straight roads.

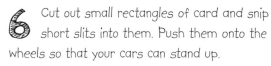
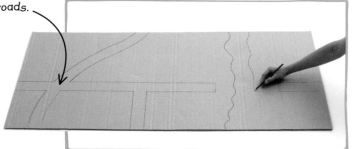

7 Paint your cars in nice bright colours, then add windows, dark-coloured tyres, and any other details you like, such as lights and bumpers.

8 Now plan out your city outline on a large sheet of thick card. Sketch out roads, rivers, and landmarks in pencil.

9 Decorate your city outline, painting in the features you sketched in **step 8**. Add green painted boxes to vary the terrain. Then arrange your cars and buildings to create a bustling scene.

Arrange your walkway so that it crosses over the road.

DOME
DEN

Have hours of fun playing outdoors or just relax and hide away in this special dome-shaped den. Once you've built your den, you can be as creative as you like when you decorate it. Paint the tiles in bold colours to make striking patterns, or even turn your den into a space base, woodland hideout, or igloo!

HOW TO MAKE A
DOME DEN

You'll be making almost 50 cardboard tiles for this dome den. Use your tile templates and make sure you measure your pieces really carefully, so that they fit together properly when you build your dome. You'll need strong tape to stick the tiles together, and lots of paint to decorate your finished dome.

You'll need a lot of cardboard, and a **spare pair of hands** to help!

Difficulty level: Hard

YOU WILL NEED

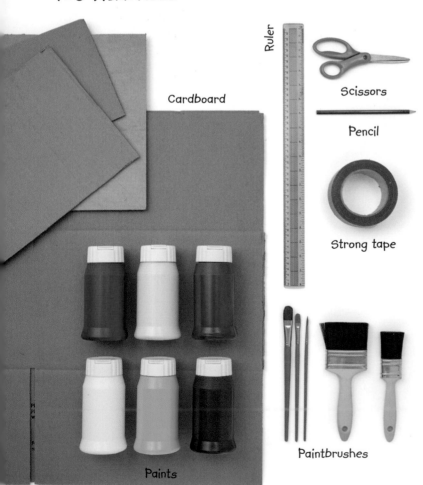

Cardboard

Ruler

Scissors

Pencil

Strong tape

Paintbrushes

Paints

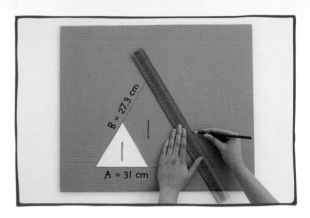

1 Lay your **triangle 1** template from page 142 on cardboard. Extend side A to 31 cm (12.2 in) and side B to 27.3 cm (10.7 in). Add a third line to complete the triangle, and cut the piece out.

B = 27.3 cm
A = 31 cm

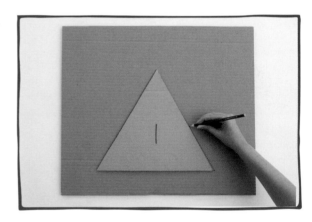

2 Lay the triangle on cardboard and draw around it to make an identical triangle.

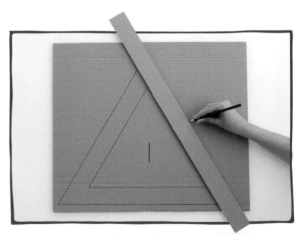

3 Make a 4 cm (1.6 in) cardboard strip and draw around it to add 4 cm (1.6 in) tab outlines to all three sides of the triangle.

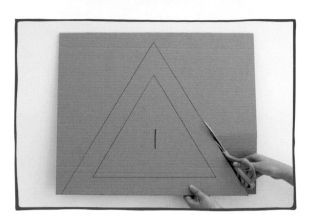

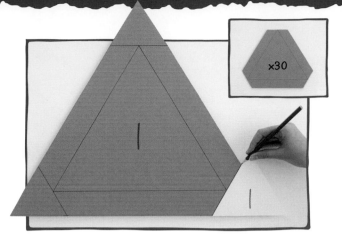

4 Cut out around the tab outlines of the triangle. This triangle will be used for your first **triangle 1 tile**.

5 Use your triangle 1 template to mark a straight line across the corners of the triangle. Cut along these lines. **Repeat steps 2-5 to make 30 triangle 1 tiles.**

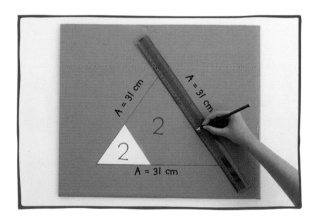

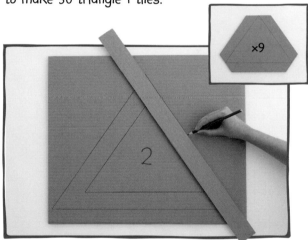

6 Now, lay the **triangle 2** template from page 143 on cardboard. Extend both sides to 31 cm (12.2 in) and join them up. Then, cut out the triangle and use it to **repeat step 2**.

7 Use the cardboard strip from **step 3** to add tabs to the triangle, then cut off the corners. **Repeat steps 6-7 to make nine triangle 2 tiles.**

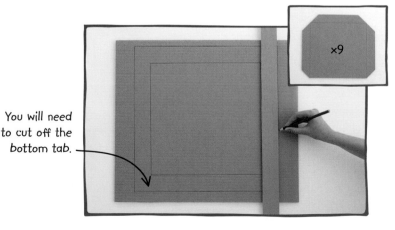

You will need to cut off the bottom tab.

8 To make your **square tiles**, draw a square on cardboard with lines that are 31 cm (12.2 in) long.

9 Use the strip from **step 3** to add tabs to the square. Use the triangle 1 template to mark and cut the corners. Then cut off the bottom tab. **Repeat steps 8-9 to make nine square tiles.**

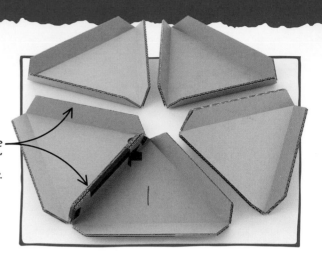

10 Score along the tab lines of all three sets of tiles. Then fold along the score lines to finish making the tabs.

11 Arrange **five triangle 1 tiles** into a pentagon shape, so the tabs on the shorter sides meet. Use strong tape to fix the first two together.

Line up the shorter "B" sides together.

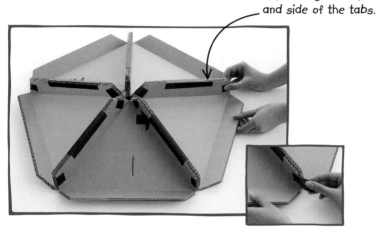

Tape along the top and side of the tabs.

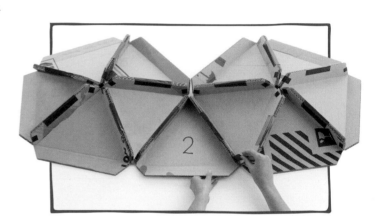

12 Secure the other edges in the same way. Then **repeat step 11** to make five more pentagons out of the remaining 25 triangle 1 tiles.

13 Now lay two pentagons next to each other, as shown, and slot a **triangle 2 tile** in between them. Tape the tabs to connect the triangle to the pentagons.

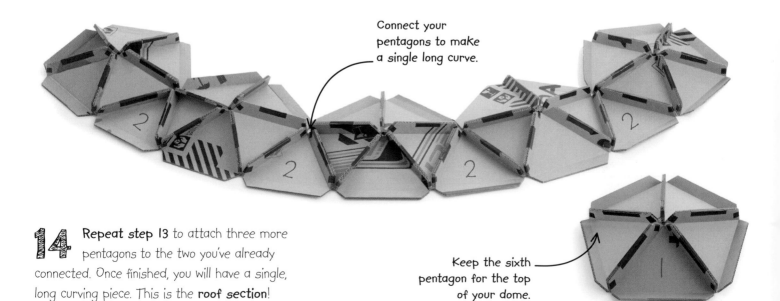

Connect your pentagons to make a single long curve.

14 Repeat step 13 to attach three more pentagons to the two you've already connected. Once finished, you will have a single, long curving piece. This is the **roof section**!

Keep the sixth pentagon for the top of your dome.

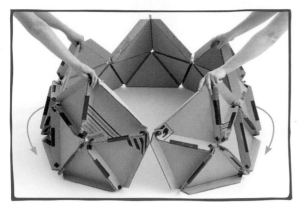

16 Slot the **five remaining triangle 2 tiles** into the V-shaped spaces around the dome's top edge. Line up the tabs and tape them together.

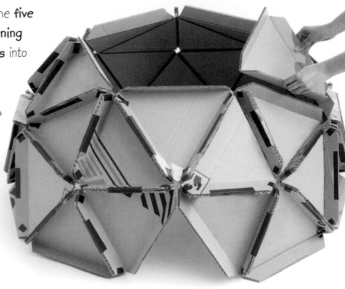

15 Stand the whole piece up and pull the ends towards each other to form a circular shape. Leave a gap at the front for the top of the door, so you can easily enter the den.

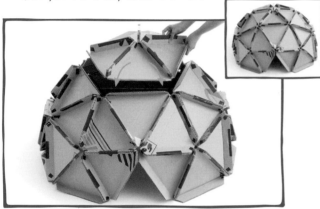

17 Place the remaining pentagon into the gap at the **top of your dome**. Tape the tabs together to complete the roof of the dome.

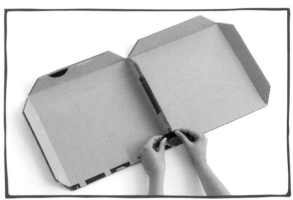

18 Now, make the **wall of your dome**. Start by taping the left-hand tab of one **square tile** to the right-hand tab of another square tile.

Ensure the remaining tabs are at the top.

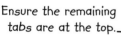

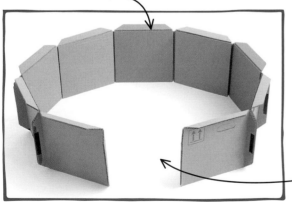

Leave a gap at the front for the entrance to the dome.

19 **Repeat step 18** to link all nine square tiles in a line. Stand the piece up and arrange it into a circle. You have now finished the wall.

Ask a friend to help you hold the roof in place.

20 Now pick up your domed roof and lower it onto the wall. Make sure the tabs on both sections line up when they meet.

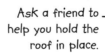

Press down on
each pair of tabs.

To keep them
steady while you add
tape, hold the tabs
in place with a
bulldog clip.

 21 Tape the wall and roof section securely
together with strong tape.

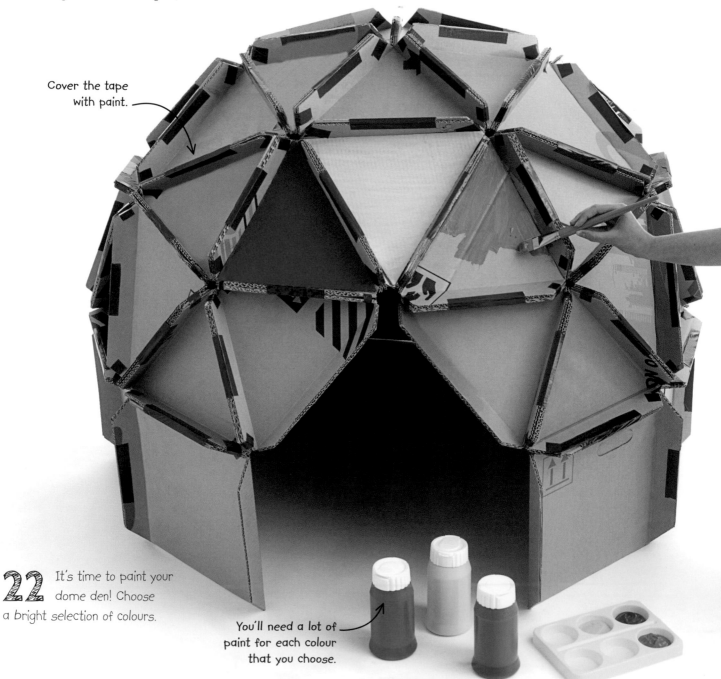

Cover the tape
with paint.

22 It's time to paint your
dome den! Choose
a bright selection of colours.

You'll need a lot of
paint for each colour
that you choose.

NOW TRY THIS

Add fairy lights to the roof of your den to make a starry ceiling, or turn your den into a space base, tortoise, woodland hideout, or igloo!

1 Use a sharp pencil to pierce holes through all the triangular roof tiles of your dome.

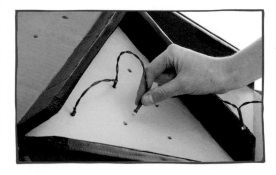

2 Take a string of battery-powered fairy lights, and push a light through each of the holes in the roof.

3 Turn the fairy lights on, and the roof of your dome will be filled with twinkling stars!

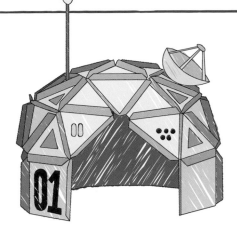

Space base
Paint your dome grey, then decorate the roof with futuristic designs. Add a satellite and an antenna to your space base.

Tortoise
First, paint the dome brown for the **shell**. Then make the **head** and **legs** and tape them to the tabs.

Woodland hideout
Decorate your dome in a green and brown camouflage pattern. Add twigs and leaves for a woodland look!

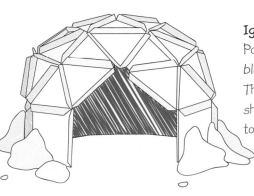

Igloo
Paint the dome in icy blue and white colours. Then stick iceberg-shaped pieces of card to the outside wall.

Turn to page 61 to find out how to make a racing helmet.

Use corrugated card to add grip to your tyres.

RECYCLED RACER

Have you ever wanted to get behind the wheel of a racing car and drive around a track at high speed? Well now you can build one that looks just like the real thing, featuring chunky tyres, a wedged-shaped nose, a cockpit you can get inside, and even a stylish spoiler at the back.

Wear the car on
your shoulders and
race your friends!

The wedged-shaped
front makes your
model look as sleek
as a real race car.

HOW TO MAKE A
RECYCLED RACER

You need lots of cardboard and strong tape for this project.
First, you'll be turning the box into the car's cockpit – the part
the driver sits inside. Then you'll be using sheets of cardboard
to build your car around the cockpit.

A **large-scale project** for the whole family to get involved in!

Difficulty level:
Hard

YOU WILL NEED

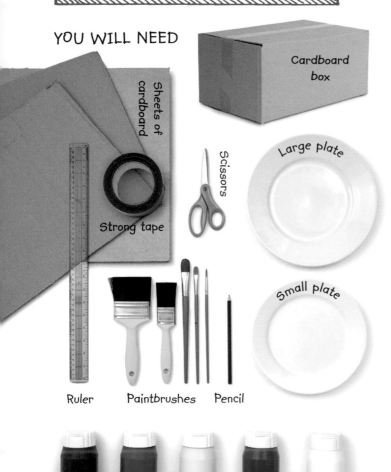

Sheets of cardboard

Cardboard box

Ruler

Strong tape

Scissors

Large plate

Small plate

Paintbrushes   Pencil

Paints

Short flap

1 To build the **cockpit**, cut a head-sized hole in the base of the box. Cut off the short flaps, too.

Keep the round piece you cut out.

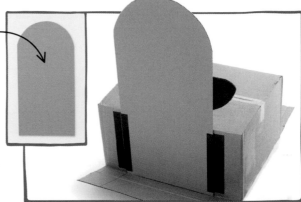

Backrest is twice the height of the box.

2 For the **backrest**, cut a cardboard piece twice the height of the box, with an arched top. Tape it to the side of the box as shown.

3 Cut slits into the ends of the flap from the edge of the box to the edge of the backrest. Score and fold each end to create tabs.

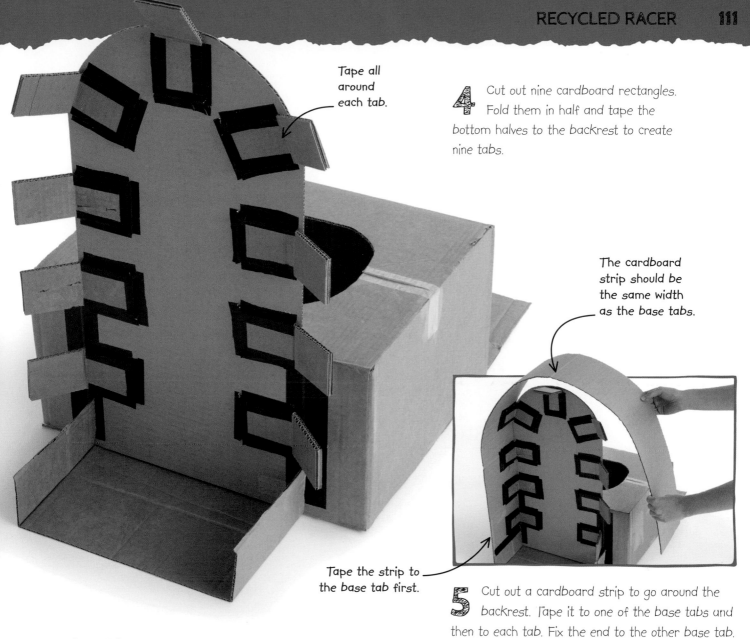

Tape all around each tab.

4 Cut out nine cardboard rectangles. Fold them in half and tape the bottom halves to the *backrest* to create nine tabs.

The cardboard strip should be the same width as the base tabs.

Tape the strip to the base tab first.

5 Cut out a cardboard strip to go around the backrest. Tape it to one of the *base tabs* and then to each tab. Fix the end to the other *base tab*.

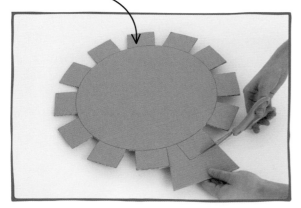

Draw tabs around the outside of the circle.

6 For the **back wheels**, draw around a large plate on cardboard. Add tabs around the circle, cut it out and fold the tabs. Repeat to make another wheel.

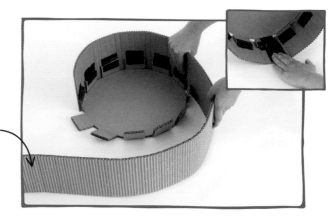

Cut strips out of corrugated card to create tyres with grip.

7 To add **tyres** to the wheels, tape a thin strip of card to the tabs on each wheel, then tape the ends of the strip together.

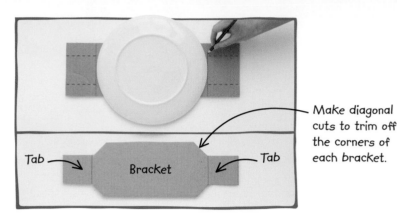

Make diagonal cuts to trim off the corners of each bracket.

Tab

Bracket

Tab

8 For the **wheel brackets**, draw around your large plate on cardboard. Add tabs to each end and cut the piece out. Repeat step to make another bracket.

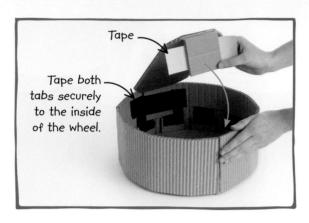

Tape

Tape both tabs securely to the inside of the wheel.

9 Tape the tabs of the brackets to the inside of the back wheel. Repeat **steps 6–9** using the smaller plate to make the **front wheels**.

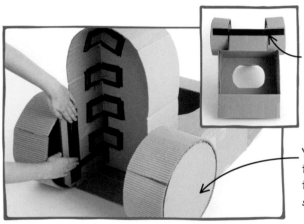

Fix tape across wheels and base for extra support.

You'll be attaching the front wheels to the car in step 22.

10 Tape the bracket of the back wheels to each side of the backrest. Then, flip the car over and tape across the base and back wheels.

Bend the strips so they bow.

11 To add **braces**, cut a long, thin strip of card and tape it from the side of the cockpit to the backrest. Fix an identical strip to the other side.

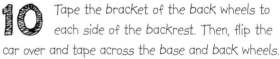

For the nose, use a sheet of cardboard that is wider than the car.

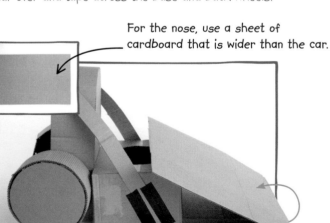

12 Now make the **nose piece**. Fold a large sheet of cardboard in half. Slide the lower half underneath the cockpit and rest the upper fold on top.

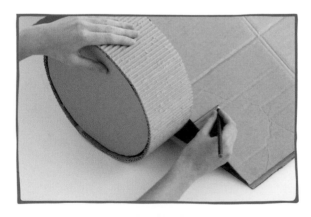

13 Hold a front wheel against the upper fold on the side of the nose piece and draw lines to mark where it sits. Repeat on the other side.

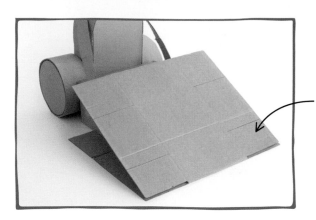

Take off the nose piece to complete marking the wheel slots.

14 Join up the two lines you've drawn on each side to make two rectangles, each one wide and deep enough for the wheels to slot into.

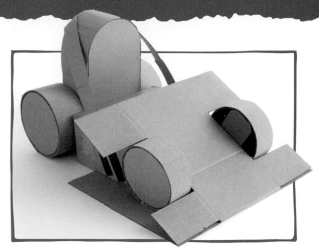

15 Carefully cut out the wheel slots with scissors. Afterwards, put the wheels into the slots to check they fit.

16 To make the car look aerodynamic, draw curves on the nose piece and in front of each wheel. Take the piece off and cut along the lines.

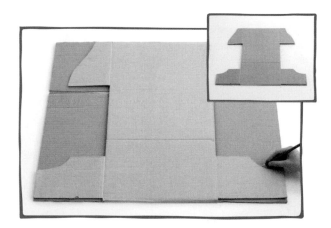

17 Now fold the piece in half and draw around the upper sheet to copy the shape onto the lower half. Cut along the lines so the two halves are the same.

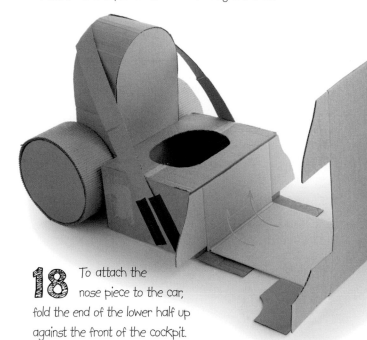

18 To attach the nose piece to the car, fold the end of the lower half up against the front of the cockpit.

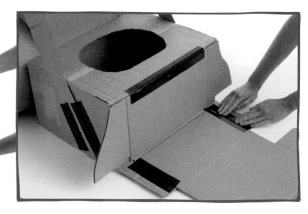

19 Tape the nose piece to the top of the cockpit and to the sides of the flap at the base of the cockpit to secure the piece to the car.

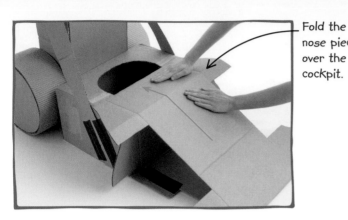

Fold the nose piece over the cockpit.

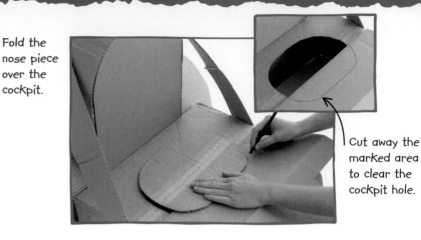

Cut away the marked area to clear the cockpit hole.

20 Fold the upper part of the nose piece over so it rests on top of the cockpit. This will cover part of the hole where your head goes.

21 Place the oval piece you cut out in **step 1** over cockpit hole. Draw around it to mark the part covering the hole, then cut it out.

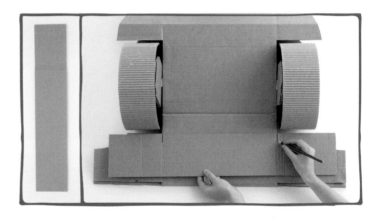

22 Tape the upper fold to the top of the cockpit. The nose piece should now fit perfectly around the cockpit hole.

23 To secure the front wheels, slot them in place first. Then lay a cardboard strip at the front and mark the distance between the inner wheel rims.

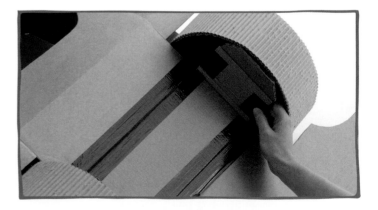

24 Fold the strip along the markings to create tabs. Place the strip on the nose in between the wheels, so the tabs align with the wheel brackets.

25 Tape the strip to the top of the car. Trim the tab ends if necessary, then tape them to the wheel brackets.

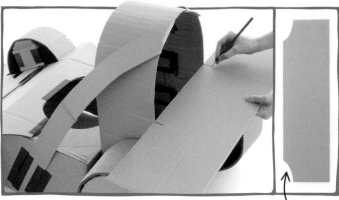

26 To add the **spoiler**, cut a cardboard strip the same length as the car's width. Hold it against the backrest and mark the slit points.

Trim the corners on one side to create the **spoiler shape**.

27 Now cut the slits, ensuring they are long enough for the spoiler to slot securely into place without touching the braces. Slide the piece in.

Number plate

Screen visor

28 Now you can add details to your car such as a **screen visor** or a circular **number plate** for the front of the car.

29 Well done! You've built your racing car. It's time to make it look fabulous by painting it in bold colours.

WILD MASKS

Get ready to tap into your wild side! With these impressive lion and zebra masks, you can dress up as two of nature's most majestic animals. The masks are ideal for a safari-themed party, or a game of chase where the lion's aim is to catch the nimble-footed zebra.

HOW TO MAKE A
LION MASK

You can either get a friend to help you build the mask around your head or build it on a balloon stand. If you decide to make a stand, blow up a balloon to roughly the size of your head and place it on a round cardboard base about the same width as your neck. This will help you make sure your mask fits you perfectly.

Take your time. Your patience will be rewarded.

Difficulty level:
Hard

YOU WILL NEED

Paintbrushes

Strong tape

Paints

Scissors

Pencil

Glue

Ruler

Cardboard sheets

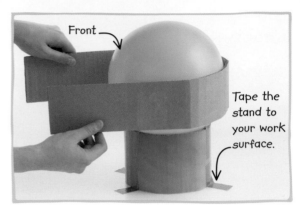

Front

Tape the stand to your work surface.

1 First, make the **frame** of the mask. Cut four strips of cardboard long enough to wrap around your head. Wrap the first strip around the middle of the balloon.

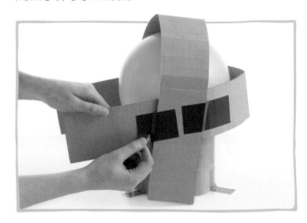

2 Wrap a second strip over the top of the balloon, so the ends are level with the base of the balloon stand. Tape the second strip securely to the first.

3 Wrap a third strip diagonally across the back of the stand so it overlaps the first two strips. Tape it to the two strips on each side as shown.

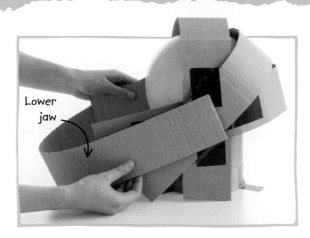

4 Loop a fourth strip across the front of the mask, positioning the ends over the third strip on each side. The fourth strip will form the lion's **lower jaw**.

Lower jaw

5 Tape the ends of the lower jaw strip securely in place on both sides. The frame of the lion mask is now complete!

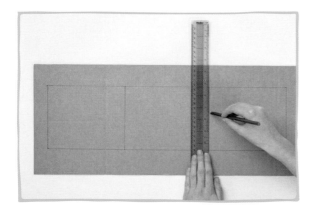

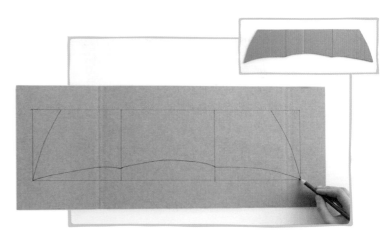

6 To make the **muzzle**, draw a rectangle about three times wider than the width of the balloon. Divide it into three equal sections.

7 Draw gentle curves across the base of each section. Then draw curves to round off the upper corners at each end. Cut the muzzle out.

The middle section of the muzzle should form a curved shape.

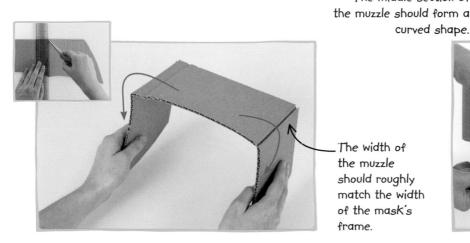

The width of the muzzle should roughly match the width of the mask's frame.

8 Use the blunt tip of your scissors to score along the two dividing lines and fold the ends down to create an n-shaped muzzle piece.

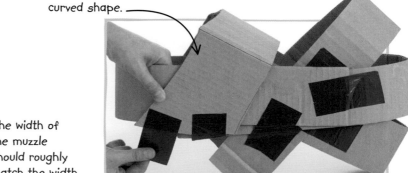

9 Position the muzzle at the front of the mask and tape the ends to the sides of the jaw strip. The top of the muzzle should be slightly curved.

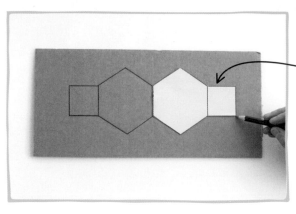

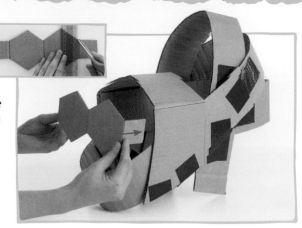

10 For the **nose**, copy the template on page 143 and draw around it on cardboard. Flip the template over and draw around it again.

You may need to alter the size of the template to make a nose piece that matches the width of your muzzle.

11 Cut the piece out. Score the ends and fold them to make tabs. Then position the nose across the muzzle and tape the tabs to either side.

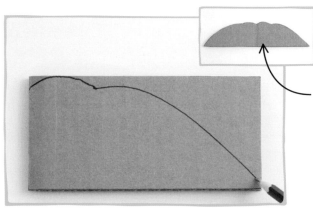

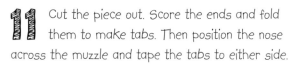

The mouth piece should look like this once you've cut it out.

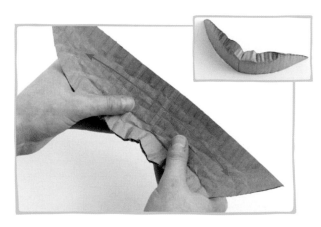

12 For the **mouth,** cut a strip of card long enough to wrap around the jaw of your mask. Fold it in half, draw the shape above, and cut it out.

13 Bend the mouth piece into a curved shape, folding in the bumpy edge to create the lion mask's bottom lip.

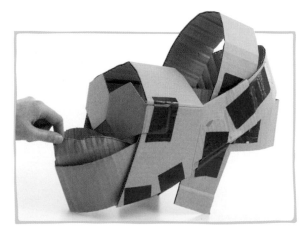

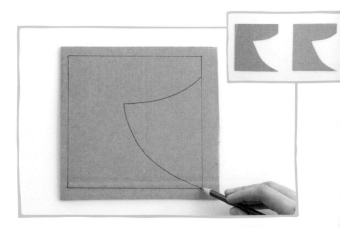

14 Tuck the mouth piece into the inside of the lower jaw with the bumpy edge facing up. Tape it to the jaw from the inside to secure.

15 For the **brows**, draw a curved triangle inside a cardboard square and cut it out. Draw around the shape to create a second, identical piece.

16 Tape the brows to either side of the mask at the top of the frame. Make sure the pointy ends are facing the front.

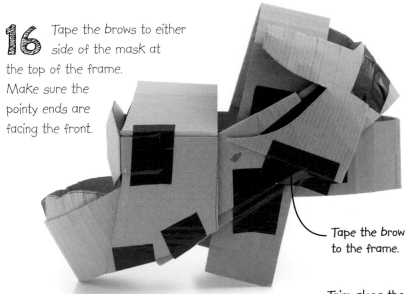

Tape the brow to the frame.

17 For the **cheeks**, draw an oval shape large enough to cover the sides of the mask from the muzzle to base of the brow. Cut the piece out.

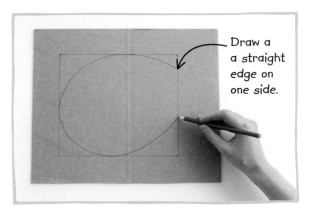

Draw a a straight edge on one side.

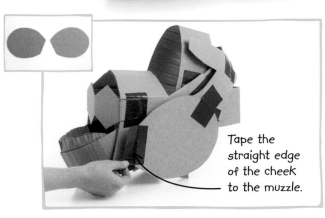

Tape the straight edge of the cheek to the muzzle.

18 Draw around the piece to make the other cheek and cut it out. Tape the cheeks to either side of the mask.

Trim along the outline of the arrowhead to make tabs with diagonal edges.

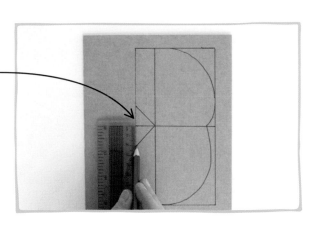

19 For the **ears**, draw a "B" inside two squares. Add a vertical line along one edge for tabs and an arrowhead across the central line. Cut the piece out.

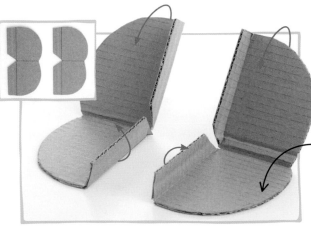

Turn one ear over before you score and fold it, so the ears mirror each other.

20 Draw around the piece to make the other ear and cut it out. Score and fold each ear along the horizontal and vertical lines.

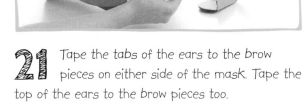

21 Tape the tabs of the ears to the brow pieces on either side of the mask. Tape the top of the ears to the brow pieces too.

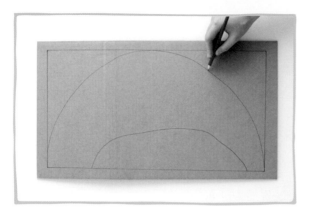

22 For the **mane**, draw a large crescent on cardboard, making it long enough to stretch from the lower jaw to the brow of the mask.

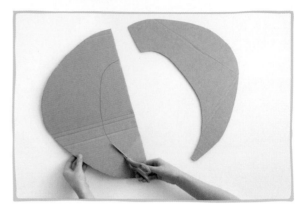

23 Cut out the shape. Then lay it on a piece of cardboard and trace around it to draw an identical piece. Cut this piece out too.

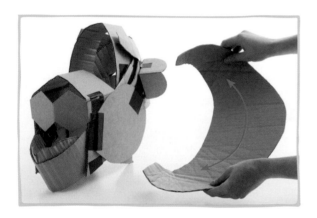

24 Bend each half of the mane into a curved shape before attaching it to the mask. If necessary, trim the inner curve for a better fit.

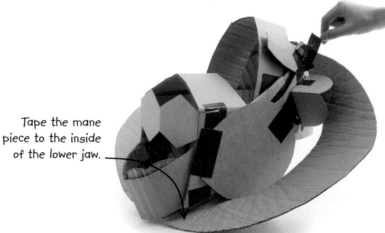

Tape the mane piece to the inside of the lower jaw.

25 Attach the mane pieces to either side of the mask by taping the ends to the brow pieces and lower jaw.

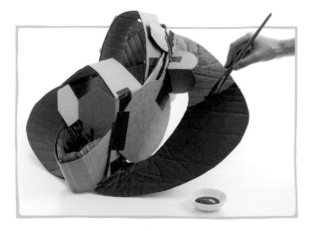

26 It's time to decorate your mask! Paint the mane in red and the rest of the mask in orange. Leave the paint to dry.

27 To complete the mane, paint a large cardboard sheet in red, orange, and yellow. Once the paint dries, cut the sheet into thin strips.

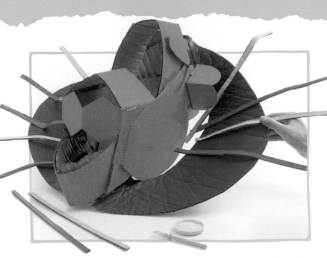

28 Glue the strips to the mane, spreading the colours evenly around the mask. Curl the ends of the strips to make the mane *big and bushy*.

29 Now add the **whiskers**. Cut out six cardboard strips with tapered ends and paint them white. Glue them to the nose as shown.

30 Your lion mask is ready to wear! As you've tailored the mask to the size of your head, it should fit perfectly.

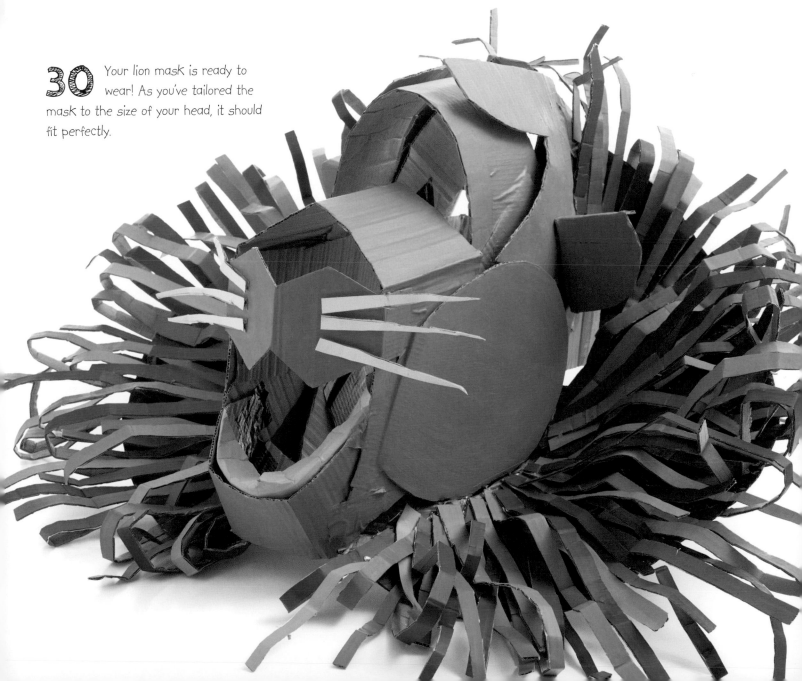

HOW TO MAKE A
ZEBRA MASK

The frame of the zebra mask is exactly the same as that of the lion mask. Once again, build the frame around your head, or on a balloon stand that roughly matches the size of your head. Then add the zebra's long nose, ears, and mane.

YOU WILL NEED

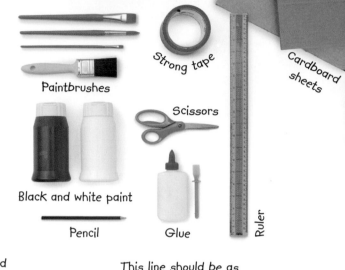

Paintbrushes

Strong tape

Cardboard sheets

Scissors

Black and white paint

Pencil   Glue   Ruler

With fewer pieces to cut, this mask should be quicker to build than the lion mask.

Difficulty level:
Medium

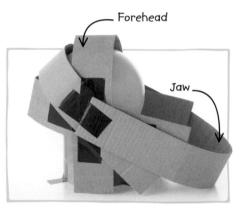

Forehead

Jaw

1 Make the **frame** of your zebra mask out of four cardboard strips, following **steps 1–4 of the lion mask**.

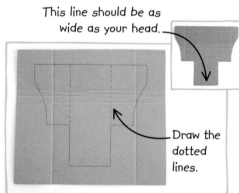

This line should be as wide as your head.

Draw the dotted lines.

2 For the zebra's **nose**, draw the above shape on cardboard, adding the dotted lines, and cut the piece out.

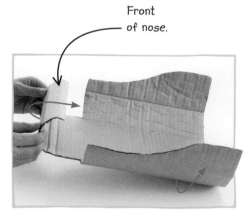

Front of nose.

3 Fold the sides of the nose along the dotted lines. Then bend the front section into a curved shape.

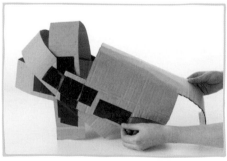

4 Flip the nose piece over and tape it to the sides of the jaw strip, making sure the curve is at the front.

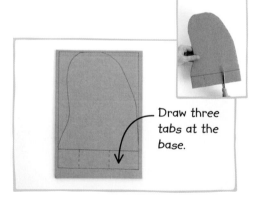

Draw three tabs at the base.

5 For the **ears**, draw the above shape with tabs at the base and cut it out. Draw around it to make an identical ear.

6 Bend the ear from both ends and bring the bottom corners together to form a funnel shape.

7 Fold out the three tabs at the base. Wrap tape around the ear, above the tabs, to secure the shape.

8 Tape the tabs of the ear to one side of the forehead strip. Repeat **steps 6–8** to add the other ear.

The inner rim needs be long enough to span the back of the mask.

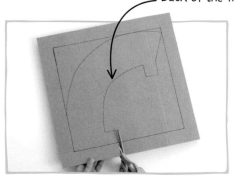

9 For the **mane**, draw a crescent on cardboard. Add tabs to the ends of the inner rim. Cut the shape out.

10 Fold the tabs in opposite directions to each other and tape them onto the mask to attach the mane.

Paint the ears white first and add the black stripes afterwards.

11 Finally, paint your mask black (except the ears) and leave it to dry. Then, paint on the white stripes. Paint the ears white and add black stripes.

Paint a white stripe around each nostril.

Leave the end of the jaw black for the zebra's mouth.

PIRATE SHIP

Transform a cardboard box into this magnificent ship, with tall masts and billowing sails. You can even make swashbuckling pirates and stand them on deck, ready for adventures and fun at sea!

Topsail

Cross spars

Main sails

Lower spars

Lower sails

Jib sails

Bowsprit

HOW TO MAKE A
PIRATE SHIP

Once you've turned a cardboard box into a sturdy structure for your ship, you'll be using lots of cardboard and garden sticks to add masts, sails, and cannons. Make sure you know what all the different parts of the ship are called – the picture on the opposite page will help you!

You'll need to **measure your sails against the masts** for a perfect fit.

Difficulty level:
Hard

YOU WILL NEED

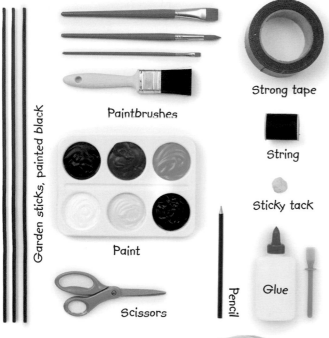

Garden sticks, painted black

Paintbrushes

Strong tape

String

Sticky tack

Paint

Glue

Scissors

Pencil

Cardboard sheet

Medium box

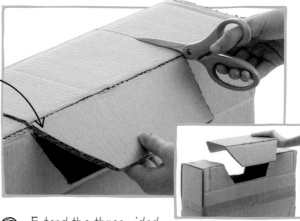

1 Draw a three-sided shape at the top of the box. Then draw a curve across one lower corner for the front of the ship and a diagonal line across the other for the rear.

Don't throw away the piece you cut out.

2 Extend the three-sided shape across the top of the box and copy it on the other side. Then cut it out and set it aside.

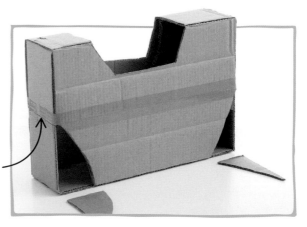

Draw lines from the top of your shapes across the width of the box.

3 Cut along the curve and diagonal line you have drawn, then cut around the edges to make two holes as shown.

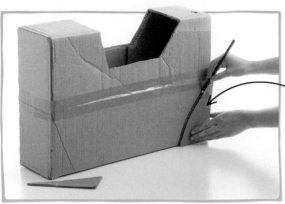

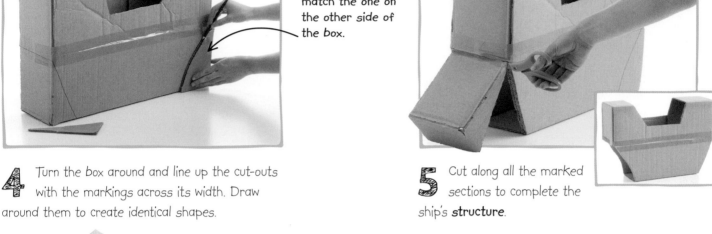

The curve must match the one on the other side of the box.

4 Turn the box around and line up the cut-outs with the markings across its width. Draw around them to create identical shapes.

5 Cut along all the marked sections to complete the ship's **structure**.

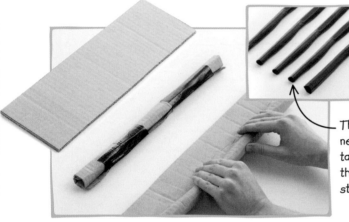

The tubes need to be taller than the ship's structure.

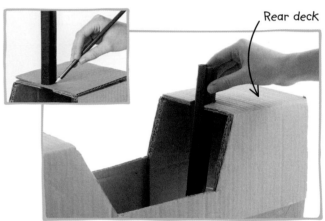

Rear deck

6 To make the **masts** and **cannons**, roll five strips of cardboard into tight tubes and secure the edges with tape, making sure they are taller than the ship's structure. Paint them all black.

7 On the inner edge of the rear deck, draw around a tube and cut out the hole. Dab glue onto the bottom of the tube. Push it into the hole and stick it to the ship's base, at a straight angle.

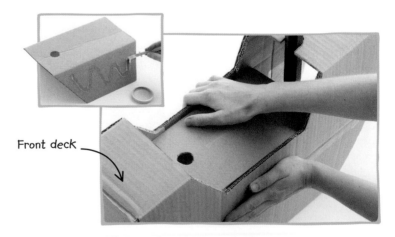

Front deck

8 Use your cut-out from **step 2** as the **main deck platform**. Place another tube near the edge of the platform, draw a circle around the tube, and cut the hole out.

9 Fold over the sides of the platform and dab glue onto them, then stick them to the inside of the ship's structure. The hole on the platform should be near the front deck.

10 Dab glue onto the bottom of the tube. Then push it into the hole to stick it to the ship's base. Your two masts are now in place.

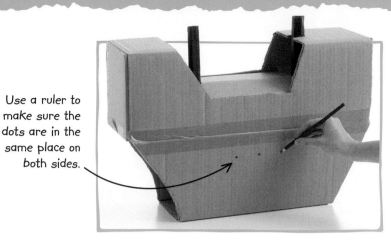

Use a ruler to make sure the dots are in the same place on both sides.

11 Use a pencil to mark three evenly spaced dots on the ship's side for the cannons. Mark dots in the same place on the other side.

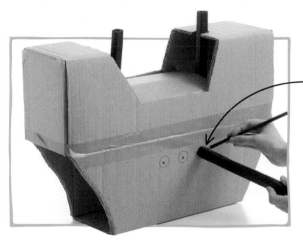

Draw around the tube over all six dots.

12 Take another tube from **step 6** and draw around it where the dots are marked. Cut out the six holes that you have drawn.

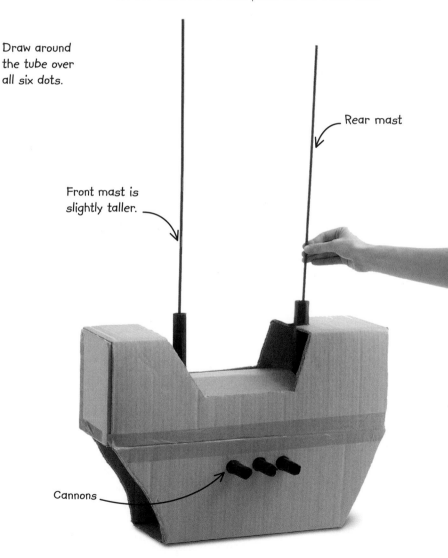

Rear mast

Front mast is slightly taller.

Cannons

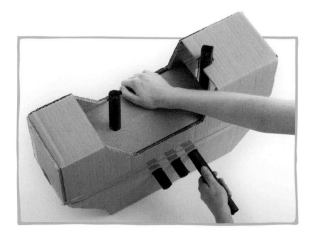

13 Push the remaining three tubes from **step 6** through the holes in the ship and out the other side. You have now made the ship's cannons.

14 To finish the masts, take two thin garden sticks about the same height as your ship. Stick them into the cardboard tubes.

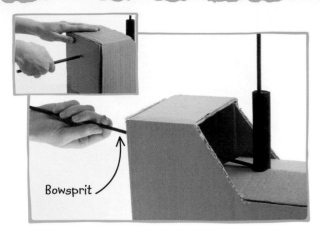

Bowsprit

15 To add the **bowsprit**, pierce a hole into the front of the ship using a pencil. Then push a garden stick into the hole, pointing up at a slight angle.

Use sticky tack to protect your fingers.

16 Now, make the **crow's nests**. Cut out two strips of card and two small circles. Put sticky tack on one side, then use a sharp pencil to pierce a hole in the centre of each circle.

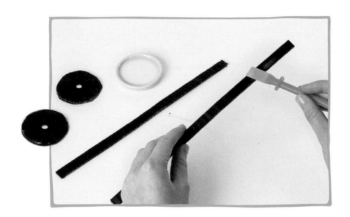

Make sure there is enough space for the sails above and below the crow's nests.

17 Paint the circles and strips of card black on both sides. Once the paint has dried, dab glue all along one side of each strip.

18 To make **bases** for the crow's nests, coil a strip from **step 17** around the rear mast about halfway up, with the glue on the inside. Repeat this on the front mast, slightly lower down.

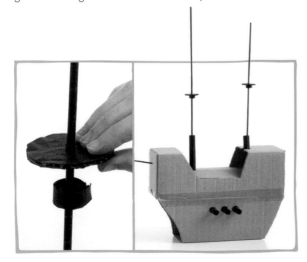

19 Slide one of your circles down the rear mast so that it sits on top of the base. Repeat the process for the front mast.

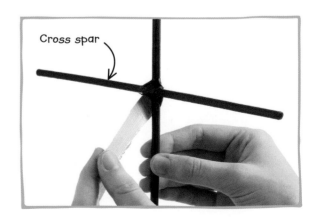

Cross spar

20 Now add the first **cross spar**. Hold a short garden stick across the front mast (slightly below the top) and secure it with tape.

21 Repeat step 20 to add another cross spar to the front mast, and a cross spar to the rear mast.

Add the second cross spar a third of the way down the front mast.

Add a cross spar slightly below the top of the rear mast.

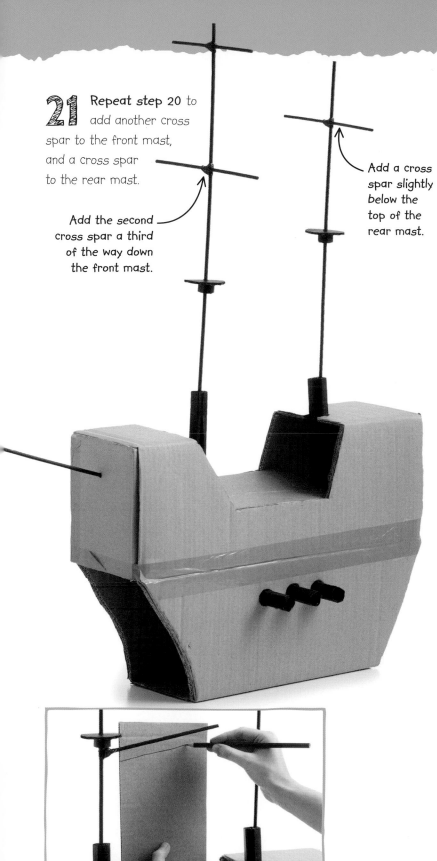

Lower spars should point to the rear of the ship.

22 Add the **lower spars** by taping short garden sticks below each crow's nest base, at right angles to the masts.

Make your sails taller than the spaces between the spars and crow's nests so they will curve out.

23 Cut out two identical cardboard rectangles for the **main sails** and a slightly smaller one for the **topsail**. Cut small grooves the same width as the garden sticks into each sail as shown.

24 To make the **lower sails**, cut out two cardboard rectangles. Line them up against the lower spars and mark the angle of the spars and where they sit. Cut along these lines.

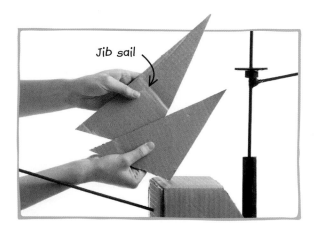

Jib sail

25 To make the **jib sails**, cut out two triangular cardboard shapes as shown that fit between the bowsprit and the front mast.

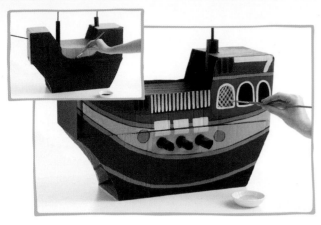

26 Now paint your ship. Apply a *base coat* of brown paint to the ship's structure. Leave it to dry, and then paint on the details.

27 Paint red and white stripes on your seven sails and leave them to dry.

Pierce holes to thread the string through.

28 Pierce holes into either corner of the longest edge of the *jib sails*. Then thread string through each hole and along the side of the sails as shown.

29 Pierce holes into both top corners and the bottom left corner of the lower sails. Thread a short piece of string through each hole.

30 Now secure your sails to the ship. First, take your *jib sails* and tie the string to the *bowsprit* and front mast.

31 Tie the top of the lower sails to the lower *spars*. Then tie the bottom left corner to each of the ship's masts.

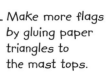

Make more flags by gluing paper triangles to the mast tops.

Pierce a hole in the ship's rear, and slide your flag into position.

32 Now attach the main sails and topsail to the masts. Bend the sails into curved shapes and use the grooves to hook them onto the masts.

33 Finally, make your **flag**. Paint a skull and crossbones onto a piece of card, with tabs as shown above, and glue it to a short garden stick.

NOW TRY THIS

Make a **crew** for your ship. Draw pirates on card, using the templates on page 144. Cut slits in the base of the pirates and use a folded strip of cardboard to stand them up.

Fold the strip for the stand in half.

Slot the ends through the slits.

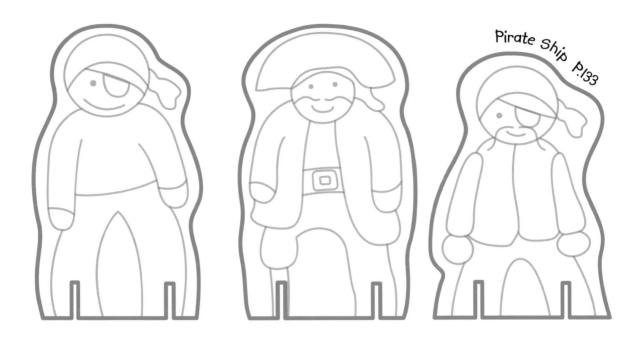

Pirate Ship P.133

ACKNOWLEDGMENTS

The publisher would like to thank the following people for their assistance in the preparation of this book: Andrew Bishop, Adam Brackenbury, Steve Crozier, Phil Fitzgerald, Tom Morse, and Stefan Podhorodecki for retouching; Gary Ombler and Howard Shooter for additional photography; Michelle Baxter, Laura Gardner, Karen Self, and Sharon Spencer for additional photography art direction; Amanda Learmonth for proofreading; Mason Beacher, Eliana Burchell, Jessica Cawthra, Kit Lane, Helen Leech, Priscilla Nelson-Cole, James Self, Kaiya Shang, Chloe Shooter, Luke Shooter, Oliver Shooter, and Jemma Westing for modelling; Felix Belfield and Jasmine Parker for assistance with the Cardville City project.

Note from the author
Thank you to the following people for their creative support and great patience over the years: Jeanette Sutton, John Archer, Scott Westing, Sophie Elder, the BrilliantBuilds crew, and, of course, my mum and dad.